Praise for Allora Dannon

"As a fellow late bloomer, I saw myself on every page. Allora names the questions so many of us carry in silence—How do I kiss someone for the first time at 30? What if I've never had sex? Am I too far behind to catch up?—and answers them with honesty, humor, and deep care."

Lily Womble, author of Thank You, More Please

"Allora's words will feel like nectar if you've felt like there was something 'wrong' with you your whole life. A must-read for anyone who feels like they're 'behind' because, spoiler alert: there's no such thing."

Lucy Meggeson, author of Thrive Solo

WHO IS SHE?

A Late Bloomer's Survival Guide

ALLORA DANNON

CARPE VITAM
PRESS LLC

To my parents, who show me daily what love is.
To every late bloomer who ever felt left behind.

Table of Contents

Chapter 1

DO IT SCARED

"Hi, I'm Allora. I'm 32. I've never been kissed, never been asked out, and never been on a date." That was how I began a series of videos that changed my life.

I am not a dating coach, a dating expert, or a matchmaker. But I do know—intimately well—how much shame and embarrassment I carried because of my forever unchosen, unkissed, unloved status. It was my most closely guarded secret.

Let me explain how I got here.

The summer I turned 32, I was tucked away in an actual castle in the Scottish Highlands for a writing retreat led by one of my favorite authors. On the last day, we were all called to gather in the "Pink Room." Its massive windows, lush cream carpets, and vintage, red-patterned couches gave the room its signature pink glow on sunny days. I sat cross-legged in the back, present but unperceived (my preference).

The retreat leaders announced that they would be giving each of the attendees an individualized parting message. My heart staccatoed. As a thriving introvert, I'd spent the week doing my best to avoid any one-on-one time with any of the leaders out of a general desire to remain unseen.

When it was my turn, my favorite author, in her signature all-black attire, looked right at me. She *saw* me. "Allora, I feel like you're letting something hold you back. And once you figure out how to let it go, your possibilities will be endless." Her words stuck with me for long after I'd gone home. She was right of course; I'd felt the truth of it in a metaphoric flash of searing heat.

I couldn't help but wonder: what couldn't I let go of?

What was I holding myself back from?

Months later, during that weird week between Christmas and New Year's, I snuggled up with my dog one morning pondering that same question. As I watched snow fall through frosted window-panes, I realized if I changed nothing, I would wake up thirty years from now and my life would look exactly the same. For the first time in my 32 years of existence, I was not okay with that.

I'd built a good life for myself. I'd accomplished things I was proud of. I loved my family, my friends, and my job. I'd traveled, pursued higher education, developed a career, and had a plethora of hobbies. But I was alone. As a child, I thought I'd be married with kids by the time I turned 25. As I got older, the lack of achieving any "normal" adult relationship milestones felt increasingly crippling. I still lived at home, I'd never so much as held some-one's hand—let alone kissed anyone—and I had no idea how to change any of it. I felt left behind, invisible, like a "failure to launch" semi-adult: mortified by my romantic inexperience, terrified of potential ridicule, and haunted by the realization that I would have traded any of my accomplishments to have found someone who loved me.

I didn't know where to start, but I was tired of being afraid of what people might think of me. I'd given this secret far too much power. So, I did what any sane millennial would do: I sat down at my desk, balanced my phone on a pile of books, and recorded the most uncomfortable admission. I struggled to say "I've never been kissed, never been asked out, and never been on a date" out loud.

I posted that confession to TikTok before I went to bed thinking that no one would ever see it. At the time, I only had a few dozen followers, I posted no regular content, and my only goal was to shed my embarrassment. I wanted to be a more honest version of myself. I didn't open TikTok again until the next day. Seated by the roaring hearth in my parents' kitchen, I was shocked when I checked my notifications to hundreds of supportive comments, over a hundred thousand views, and a follower count that rapidly kept rising as the day wore on: 1000, 8000, 10000.

Complete strangers, many with similar life experience, expressed support, understanding, and surprise that many fellow late bloomers existed. I started posting video after video, commiserating with the shared frustrations, heartache, and isolation of chronic singleness. Romance, relationships, sexuality—universal experiences that many people had no experience with, felt deep shame over, and all without realizing that others struggled with the same issue as well. By the end of two weeks, my follower count jumped over thirty thousand. Newspapers, magazines, and radio stations started reaching out for interviews. Suddenly, I was on a soap box broadcasting what had been my most carefully guarded secret, and people were not only listening, but many also felt uniquely seen and understood.

The term "Late Bloomer" can be applied to anyone who finds success in anything later in life. For me, it specifically applied in the romance department—as if everyone else in the world had figured out relationships/dating/love, but I'd somehow missed the boat. Worse, I didn't know what I'd done wrong. Dating seemingly happened organically for everyone else. I didn't know how to make it happen for me.

Dating, after all, is a terrifying prospect with unknown results. In every other area of my life (career, education, travel, hobbies, etc.), there was a positive result for my effort. Dating had no such guarantee.

That snowy morning, I realized two things:

- No knight in shining armor was coming to save me from my isolation.

- I'd been operating under an insane myth: that one day I was just going to *feel* ready.

I'd been waiting for this magnetic sweep of inspiration and confidence and a spontaneous combustion of all my fears. I had been waiting to feel brave.

But that thing you're desirous of? Fearful of? Longing for? You know the one. You're unlikely to ever feel 100% ready to take that initial leap into achieving it.

In December, when I redownloaded a dating app for the tenth time in as many years, it was the last thing I felt like doing. To hold myself accountable, I made two personal promises:

- Since I was unlikely to ever feel ready, do it scared.
- Bravery is exhausting. Don't quit, just rest when you need it.

Learning to date in my thirties was terrifying. I'd gone unnoticed for my entire adulthood, and I'd also gotten good at avoiding things I deemed scary. In order to trick myself into not chickening out after a week or two (my M.O. for the last decade), I decided I would document my journey and talk about my experience (or lack thereof) until this was just another fact about me, like my height or hair color.

It's some kind of cosmic joke that I would become an unofficial late bloomer spokesperson after that first video, that the first person to ask me out on my first ever date would be lovely, that my life would change in every conceivable way, that I would fall in love.

Admittedly, this is not a love story. It is, a little, about finding a partner, but not to "complete me." This is a story about letting go of fear, curbing the insecurities that held me back from experiencing all life has to offer, and, most importantly, about finding myself. Even though I am in no way professionally qualified to give relationship advice, I did learn a few things. Most important of all? That I'd rather try and fail than spend my whole life waiting for what I want to find me. That's why I want to share this story with you.

Whether you are a late bloomer, chronically single, or simply looking for a change: you cannot be late for your own life. Everything you're afraid of could happen, but everything you're hoping for could happen, too. You'll probably never feel ready for that thing that will change your life.

So, let's be terrified together.

Do it scared.

Chapter 2

WHY WERE YOU A LATE BLOOMER?

The afternoon sun silhouetted my little sister where she stood in the middle of the barn aisle. It caught her hair—curly, like mine, but always pulled into a tight ponytail—as we mucked horse stalls. She was maybe eleven or twelve, I was thirteen, and she'd been passed a letter by a friend. She'd looked up at me, smiled, and said, "Michael likes me."

My cheeks burned as I paused to lean on my pitchfork and tried to look uninterested. "Do you like him back?" I asked, aiming for something like nonchalance.

She shrugged. "He's always liked me."

There were three boys around her age at our local home-school group, and all three had liked her at some point. I wish I remembered giggling with her, talking about her favorites amongst them—who'd she choose (if any). She was warm with other people. I didn't understand how it came so naturally to her while I felt increasingly invisible. All I remember thinking was how —*how*—did she know how to do that? How did she get boys to notice her?

And why had it never happened to me?

When people ask me why I was a late bloomer, they expect this clear "Aha!" moment where I pinpoint the reason. For instance, I was the oldest of ten homeschooled kids.

I'll stop you right there. You just formed an image, right, of what that meant my childhood looked like? A snap judgment about how I grew up? That I must have been unsocialized and awkward? Maybe.

My parents were both children of broken homes and alcoholic fathers. They wanted to create a stable, loving, supportive life for us that they didn't necessarily have growing up—a little oasis where we were loved, our creative interests were nurtured, and where we'd grow into confident, accomplished, well-educated individuals. As much as they wanted to shelter us from the world, they also wanted to prepare us for it. We met up regularly with other homeschooled kids, volunteered at nursing homes, joined sports teams and various clubs, travelled—visiting historical sites around the country and broadening our worldviews. We took etiquette and small talk classes. A few of us even did some competitive public speaking, myself included. My dad would coach us after work.

We made friends. We assimilated into society. My siblings and I grew up close, encouraged but not pressured, sheltered but not naïve. It wasn't without its trials, but, all in all, it was a beautiful way to grow up.

All of us went to college—some, like me, graduating early at nineteen. Do that math. I was fifteen when I started college (something far more uncommon for homeschoolers back then). You might be thinking—oh yes, that's it! Again, maybe. From day one on a college campus, I felt like a fish out of water. Everyone was years older, and I desperately wanted to fit right in. If anything, starting college early developed one of my favorite skills: becoming a social chameleon.

Within a semester or two, I learned how to dress like a college student (Aughts Uniform: hoodie, North Face fleece, Uggs, flare jeans) and how to talk like one. I googled terms I didn't know and formed all kinds of opinions on super important topics like 69ing (too much work) or blowjobs (messy but not unwelcome). As I continued my college education, I learned how to empathize with friends going through breakups, first dates, hookups, parties. I didn't outright lie, but I always made it a point to make anyone think I knew what they were talking about.

Although my lack of experience felt a little uncomfortable as a teenager, it didn't start to bother me until I graduated with my Masters at 22. None of my other siblings had this same struggle. All of them dated in college, some marrying their partners not long after graduating. As each of my siblings coupled up, I couldn't help but wonder: where had I gone wrong? Had they all taken a class I'd somehow missed?

Worse, I'd never heard of anyone like me, and I wouldn't until I turned 30.

That is a long time to carry a secret you can't bear to say out loud, to feel like you are the only one who's watching such an intrinsic part of life pass you by. It would have changed my life to know that my lack of romantic experience was far more common than most people realized.

I've been asked many times if there are any common threads amongst the late bloomer community. Although there are an infinite number of reasons that someone does not pursue dating, there are a few commonalities many of us share:

1. **We feel invisible**.

No one paid us any romantic attention. The longer you go without that kind of attention, without learning how to date or to flirt, without feeling perceived or hitting those milestones at a "nor-mal" age, the more alien you feel. The longer you carry the belief that you must be an unlovable, grotesque monster, the more your shame and embarrassment compound. The more you witness the organic growth of relationships around you, the more impossible it feels to ever be in one yourself. It's a brutal cycle. And because you don't see or hear about other people with your lived experience outside of mainstream "virgin" or "cat lady" jokes, you retreat further into your own isolation and shame. Or, at least, that's what happened for me as I watched every single one of my younger siblings (all nine of them) couple up, along with all my cousins, friends, co-workers, etc. until there was just me. Forever alone.

2. **Dating feels unknown and stressful, so you just avoid it entirely**.

Dating requires bravery. It's a vulnerable process, offering your heart to a stranger and asking them to "please, handle this with care." But there is a certain misconception that because late bloomers crave relationships and have never had them before, that they must be living miserable lives. Not so. Is there sometimes an acute, unbearable loneliness? Absolutely. But many late bloomers have simply invested their time and energy into building lives they love instead. They focused on hobbies, friendships, jobs, education, travel—things that require risk and work, but have more predictable (and rewarding) outcomes which correlate to the time and energy you put in. The intimidating thing about dating is that you can do absolutely everything right: present the best version of yourself, actively "put yourself out there," implement all the dating advice, and still come back empty-handed.

When people ask me "why were you a late bloomer," they are expecting a straightforward answer—a single reason or traumatic event to account for me missing out on such a normal part of the human experience. There isn't a single big reason, just a whole mix of insecurities and fears that worsened over time.

Here are a few others to toss into the mix:

1. Anytime I admitted my late bloomer background to any potential connection (usually through a dating app), the responses were fairly lackluster and did little to encourage continued effort.
2. As a plus-sized woman, I had a lot of anxiety especially over not being deemed attractive to anyone else. My parents tried to instill in me that I was more than my physical appearance, but there was no amount of self-esteem to counter the shallowness of modern dating

culture. Having existed in a plus-sized body my entire adult life, I knew how the world (generally speaking) felt about fat people. My dread of navigating modern dating, with its focus on physical attraction, was only heightened by my own insecurities. It felt like it would chip away at the self-esteem I'd built up on my own, brick by brick. Why risk it?

3. I had no life experience to draw from. Although I knew no one was born knowing how to navigate relationships, I felt behind. I didn't know how to flirt. I didn't know how to be sexy. I didn't know how to attract a partner, and I had no idea how to "practice" any of those things. Dating can be intimidating when you have no idea what you're doing, at an age when it is socially expected of you to have figured it all out a long time ago.

4. As a straight woman, I struggled with the concept of dating safety. I read that one of the biggest fears most men have with online dating is being catfished. For women or queer folk, it's being assaulted, raped, and/or murdered. An excellent reason to not try at all.

5. Despite bouts of loneliness, I had built a life I loved—a life I was proud of. I didn't know how someone would fit into it. I didn't know if I wanted to give up my time, and I couldn't imagine wanting to devote so much energy to something so unknown and unpredictable. Was this worth upsetting what was already working for me?

All of that fear boiled down to this: forcing myself to pursue dating didn't feel worth the risk. Instead, I let my childhood dreams of finding romance fade with each passing year. I learned how to adventure alone. I learned how to live an independent, fulfilling life outside of anyone else's needs. It wasn't until that holiday week in 2022 that I realized nothing would change if I changed nothing. For the first time, I wasn't okay with that.

I was waiting for my big dreams of romance to just come find me which didn't make any sense. Anything else I had achieved or pursued in my life hadn't landed in my lap. I'd fought, sacrificed, and persevered for it all. Nothing worth having was free.

I couldn't help but wonder: why couldn't I approach dating like that, too?

The why didn't really matter; what I was going to do about it now did.

Chapter 3

YOU JUST HAVE TO PUT YOURSELF OUT THERE

If you've been single for any length of time (but most especially, you know, for your entire life) there are a series of less than helpful comments you've likely run into:

Have you tried putting yourself out there?

Out where? Where was I supposed to be going? I'd gone to college and started working straight after graduation. I'd gone through a "download a dating app / get creeped out or overwhelmed within two weeks / delete dating app" cycle for a literal decade without any positive results. I was tormented with the notion that I was too late for the entirety of romantic experience. Was I not social enough? I did, admittedly, enjoy mostly solo hobbies (reading, hiking, writing), but I'd been on a team in college, I'd gone to parties, I'd made friends. I'd been "out" living my life at a brisk, fulfilling pace, but I'd never been hit on, never asked out, never passed notes in school by secret admirers. No one had ever noticed me.

You'll find love when you least expect it.

At this point, I'd been expecting to die alone. You can't "least expect" it more than that. I knew people were trying to remind me that, in the words of the great Dr. Ian Malcolm, "Life finds a way." But with every year of my life that passed, it was becoming increasingly clear that no one was coming to find me. I didn't have a "meet-cute" story like my parents who met in high school. My nine younger siblings had no problem going out on first dates, having first kisses, or getting married. In fact, by the time I turned 32, my youngest sister—age 16—had already moved on to her second boyfriend.

I didn't understand. I was smart. I was adventurous. I'd been on several international trips, loved hiking, and had learned to travel solo. I was successful—I'd run an online clothing boutique for years and developed a fashion obsession as a result. I was driven, creative, and determined to chase my dreams of publication. I loved who I was. I loved my life. There was plenty of room to share it with somebody else. So why did I feel invisible? Where was my moment of serendipity? What was I doing wrong? It was a question that haunted me with every passing year, and it was a pain no one around me seemed to understand.

You need to love yourself first.

I understood this advice to a point: there is merit in not waiting for someone else for your life to begin. To paraphrase Shani Silver, my single life was not a prologue. I loved the life I'd built and the people in it. But building a life I loved and was proud of hadn't gotten me any closer to finding a partner. All it had done was cement that I was better off on my own. Who was worth potentially disrupting my peace? There were too many unknowns in romance to justify risking it all, so why bother?

What bothered me the most about this advice was the implication that coupled folk had no self-loathing or self-hatred. That they had all met up as fully formed, fully healed, fully ready human beings that were worthy of companionship. Did I want to be the best version of myself? Absolutely. Did my own insecurities, self-esteem issues, or trauma responses mean I was doomed to be forever alone?

Absolutely not.

The suggestion, even offered lovingly, haunted me. How could I ever reach this elusive standard for dating, if that standard meant I had to be perfectly at peace with myself?

You're so pretty/cool/smart/funny/etc., why are you still single?

This one is tricky because it's swaddled in an unintentionally back-handed compliment. The speaker is acknowledging your best qualities, marveling that someone with your beauty/charisma/humor/intelligence/etc. could—thus far—be undiscovered by a potential suitor. However, in that acknowledgement there's also the unspoken implication of: "If you have these great qualities, then what else is wrong with you?"

Most people want to be kind and sympathetic. They want to take the sting out of what you already know: that someone should love you for who you are, because you're already awesome. The implication otherwise used to keep me awake at night, inventorying all my flaws.

Have you prayed about it?

I grew up Roman Catholic, which meant that prayer was—and still is—built into the action items I took when approaching any problem or pain point. But what if the Almighty was taking his sweet time with a request that seemed easy peasy for everyone else *except* you? What if your prayers on this subject, for whatever reason, feel like they're sliding straight to voicemail? What if you've been praying for *years* and nothing has changed?

It's another kind of comment with a hurtful underside. If you had prayed more or believed harder, your faith would have been rewarded, your dreams of romance and love would have come true

14

sooner. No matter how you paint this one, it can still sting, even when asked from a loving place.

Have you tried the dating apps?

I promise you, at this point, every single person knows what online dating is and has tried the apps (probably multiple times). We can tell you what we like/dislike about each one. It is difficult to market yourself and make connections on platforms designed to keep people using them for as long as possible.

Can we learn to leverage our profiles/interactions better for our own mental sanity and for a chance at better results? Of course. Alternatively, we've heard so many horror stories about online dating that we're now avoiding all the apps like the plague. All-in-all? This isn't the solution people thing it is—especially when they've likely never needed to use an app themselves to meet their own partners.

You're so lucky / you're not missing much.

My mother has always been something of a Pollyanna. It's a trait I've inherited from her: always trying to find the silver lining in any situation. She's told me I was lucky, blessed even, for being able to live my life without heartbreak or attachments, that I was missing out on the pain and hardship having a partner could cause. My mother was trying to remind me of the big life I had lived, all the adventures I'd gone on, all I had accomplished, all the people who already did love me. But I didn't feel lucky. I felt alone.

Until I turned 30, I thought I was the only person in the world with my experience. I'd never heard the term "late bloomer" and had, most definitely, never heard of anyone talking about a lack of romantic experience in a normalized way. It wasn't until I joined TikTok in 2020 that I heard two other content creators, Britt Belwine and Kendra Okereke, talk about their experiences as romantic late bloomers for the first time. I had no idea that there were more people like me. I'd felt adrift my entire adult life, lost at sea without a life preserver. It was a special kind of isolation. As I watched everyone around me couple up, celebrating engagements, weddings, baby showers, etc., I didn't feel lucky. I felt alien. And I wanted just one person, any person, to acknowledge that hurt and how hard it was to live with.

IN ANY OF THESE SCENARIOS:

A response along the lines of "I'm so sorry you've had that experience. It sounds really hard/painful," would have been a balm for my soul. Unless I was outright seeking advice, I just wanted my isolation validated. At the end of the day, I promise you, most late bloomers don't want to talk about their relationship status unless they explicitly bring it up. Remember: no one is owed your life story. There is nothing wrong with you. You are worthy of every dream you've ever dreamt.

You are worth more than your experience or lack thereof. You have so much to give to yourself and to other people. You are worthy, loveable, and simply on your own timeline. You can't be late to your own life. And if you want to brave the horrors of online dating, there's a few things I've learned about that, too.

Chapter 4

PROBABLY FATTER IN REAL LIFE

The Situation:

Online dating, as a whole, can be such a clusterfuck.

It comes down to luck, good marketing, persistence in your efforts, and to somehow not let the whole process hurt your feelings. Easy, right? Each app/site has its own quirks, gimmicks, algorithms, dating pools, and interface. Each is designed to encourage your usage for inordinate amounts of time and, most importantly, to buy into the "premium features" that will, supposedly, help give you access to "better matches." With that said, dating apps *are* a tool for meeting people and, for better or worse, they were the only way I was interested in "putting myself out there."

As a late bloomer, downloading a dating app was especially intimidating because I'd gotten comfortable with being invisible. Yet there I was, setting up a profile with the explicit intention of being seen and worse—*trying* to attract a partner. I had to figure out how to communicate my whole personhood and why someone should date me, all through a series of prompts, coy phrasing, and curated pictures. I was, essentially, creating an advertisement for myself as a potential life partner. That's not daunting at all.

I didn't know how to flirt. Although I had a healthy dose of self-esteem, I had no idea if I had a sexy bone in my body. Over the ten-odd years that I downloaded the various apps, setting up a new profile felt torturous every time. Even though I despised them, there was no denying that, as a tool, they were the least invasive option for changing my circumstances.

The Plan:

This time however, unlike every other time I'd tried, I made myself three critical promises:

1. I would brave the dating app hellscape and give them my all for a finite period of time—a "Season of Bravery." I was determined to nurture every conversation that had potential (a.k.a. anyone who matched my conversational energy in getting to know them without being creepy, invasive, or overwhelming), and say yes to every non-red-flag opportunity to go on a date. I set a goal to go on eight dates by Easter (roughly three and a half months).
2. Unlike the other times I'd dabbled in dating apps—I would rest, but not quit, if things weren't going my way. I could be brave, but not forever. If I didn't see any positive outcomes by the end of my "Season of Bravery," I would take a break and try again later.
3. No one was owed an explanation of my lack of romantic history until I was ready to share it with them. Over the years, my late bloomer status was something I'd attempted to confess immediately. People's reactions were mixed, and usually so disheartening that it would scare me off. Those reactions generally fell into one of four categories:
   a. The Aladdin: Responds with "Let me show you a whole new world … [insert some sexual innuendo that would overwhelm or underwhelm me]."

b. The Ghost: Immediately ignores your most vulnerable admission and is never heard from again.
c. The Trauma Inquisitor: Asks "Why? What's wrong with you? What happened?" You know, super light conversation—getting drilled for your entire traumatic backstory from a total stranger.
d. The Mature Adult: Once in a while you stumble across these gems who take this in stride with tact and poise. They were, in my experience, rare.

When I realized that someone else's reaction was an amazing red flag/green flag test in and of itself, it started to take the edge off. You can learn so much about a person based off of how they react to you.

You might be asking: what would I say instead?

"I do not have a lot of dating experience."

The End.

REMEMBER, no one is owed your life story unless you feel comfortable sharing it. We are not revealing a deep, dark secret (even though it feels like it). Being a late bloomer is just a state of being. It should have the same impact as telling someone your favorite color or where you grew up. I know it's not that easy. You're also battling cultural stigma and people generally sucking ass. You can't change that some people may judge you. The only thing you can change is how *you* judge you. I'm telling you right now, babe, you've carried the shame of this long enough. Try setting it down for a while and see how that feels. You might be surprised by how much lighter you feel once you let it go.

Let's tackle the first scary part together: setting up a bitchin profile.

Build a Bitchin Profile

The advice that's out there for what works on dating apps is vast and varied. I'd like to preface this section by saying I am not a dating coach or a dating app guru. What I am is a gal who's used a lot of apps and who has worked in marketing for the last ten plus years. These are observations collected from my own time in the trenches.

Most importantly, success depends on timing, alignment of intention, marketing yourself well, and algorithms. It has absolutely **nothing** to do with you being worthy of love. Throw that last misconception away—**it's not true**. If you don't get the opportunities you're looking for, you can make adjustments and try again. Remember, this is just the presentation of the information with the goal of hitting the right audience, not a measurement of your worth or desirability.

I formatted my most recent dating profiles with a few guiding principles in mind:

1. **Don't be boring**.

   Now is not the time to be mysterious or an enigma. Answer the dumb prompts, talk about your personality, interests, aesthetic—your life! You are looking for someone that's compatible with your interests. Have some and don't be shy about sharing them. The more detail you include, the more it gives observant matches something to start a conversation.

EXAMPLES FROM MY OWN PROFILE:

I GEEK OUT ON:
"Elvis, reading (mostly SciFi/Fantasy), hiking (currently building up to higher altitude hikes!), travel (I'm always planning my next

trip), gardening, beekeeping, and movies (Marvel/Star Wars, Jurassic anything.)"

TYPICAL SUNDAY:

"When the weather is nice: hiking with my dog, gardening, or working my family's farm. During the winter I tend to be a book gremlin and try to have fun in the snow. I also love going out to try new foods."

2. **Be upfront about what you are looking for—not what you think people are looking for**.

Much of online dating revolves around hookup culture or people misrepresenting their intentions. If you're looking for something long-term, say that. The goal here is not to make yourself desirable to everyone, it's to hone in on your target audience (a.k.a. someone who wants to date you).

3. **Use good pictures**.

You want to market yourself to a targeted audience. You're trying to narrow your options down to a good match. As Lily Womble says, "Appeal to the few, not the many." With that said, here are a few suggestions for posting better pictures:

- **You have a split second to get someone's attention**.

How you choose to do that is up to you, but for me, the first picture you post of yourself should be of **just you** in **bright, clear lighting**.

- **The easiest way to take a good picture**?

Do your hair/makeup/whatever makes you feel fabulous, face a window for the natural light, and take a selfie. Want a full body shot but too shy to ask a friend to take one of you? Take a picture in a full-body mirror. Don't have a full-body mirror? Go find a dressing room with decent lighting and take one there. I always loved Torrid and Old Navy mirrors. This is your first chance to get someone's attention. I know you're a cutie. When in doubt: don't underestimate the power of a cute mirror selfie!

Me during Fashion Week

- **Let your next pictures introduce your life, your pets, your interests, your home, your travels, etc**.

Don't skip the opportunity to share a glimpse of your life with someone.

- **Pictures with other people are distracting (exception: unless you have kids)**.

We don't want to have to do detective work to figure out which person in a group picture you are. If you include a group picture, let it be ONLY one. And if there is a child in your photo, please explain them.

Take me back to

Are you a dog person because

4. **Don't be afraid to hype up your best qualities**.

You are marketing yourself, remember? As an example, I talked about my propensity for honestly, loyalty, and loving outdoor/farm life. You are introducing yourself and targeting someone who also values those qualities. It could be something silly, too. I, for instance, was drawn to my first ever date's profile with a silly line in his intro paragraph: "I have broad shoulders to cuddle with in front of a roaring fire." Cheesy? Yes. But did I love the mental image of that cheesiness? Also yes. Did I start picturing myself with him in front of that roaring fire? You bet your bottom dollar I did. That mental image felt specifically targeted for me. Remember, preferences are subjective. What I find attractive could be a huge turn off for someone else. The point still stands: *be yourself*! There's someone out there who has been looking for exactly what you have to offer.

5. **Mix it up**.

Not getting any engagement with your profile? Try switching up your photos, trying new prompts, or rewording your intro. In marketing, we call this 'A/B Testing.' Essentially, we try out a few different phrases/images/etc. conveying the same message at a time and see what is more successful. We experiment with different factors to encourage different results. There is always an alternate way to present the same information. Not getting great engagement? Pivot from your current strategy and try something new. **This does not mean you are unworthy of love or that no one will ever be attracted to you**. You simply haven't figured out the right messaging or presentation to attract your target audience yet, AND you're battling an algorithm that really wants you to pay for more exposure.

6. **Don't like one app? Try another**.

I found it overwhelming to use more than two apps at once. However, you might get zero traction on one app and much better engagement on another. So many apps are out there and vary by user base and location. Don't like Hinge? Try Bumble. Don't like Bumble, try Tinder. The goal is to not overwhelm yourself, but to give yourself more options.

7. **Best Practices**:

In addition to the promises I made myself during my dating journey, I also decided on a few "Best Practices" to help protect my mental health.

1. **Small talk sucks. Make your conversations count**. Look, I get it. Pushing through the banality of small talk is one of the seven circles of hell. It's hard to care about someone without knowing them, so get to know them. Google meatier questions if you need ideas. I usually give a conversation two to three rounds to see if someone is going to put in some effort, otherwise "bless and release" those who do not match your energy (another concept from Lily Womble's *Thank You, More Please*).

2. **Don't pre-judge what someone else will be attracted to**. It's impossible to know what a stranger might be into or who they are looking for. I found myself pre-judging if a match could be attracted to me (especially as a plus-sized girlie), and would shoot them down before even trying, because I decided that FOR them. ALLORA, WHY? This is what I mean. There's no way of knowing what's in someone's heart or soul without getting to know them—so know them (and THEN feel free to judge).

3. **Stop making snap judgments**. You could be swiping past something great because of snap judgments you don't realize you're making. For example, although I love to wear flannel and I grew up in the country—on a literal farm—I automatically rejected any match wearing flannel because my judgey self was convinced it was a sign that they were "too" country. Want to guess what my first ever date was wearing in his first profile picture on Hinge? FREAKING FLANNEL. I had skipped right by his profile not once, *but twice*, because of a stupid snap judgment. Similarly, that same date admitted that he made snap judgments about my tattoos. If he'd realized I had tattoos before our date, he wouldn't have asked me out. We would have both missed out on one of the biggest adventures of our lives if we hadn't broadened our perceptions.

4. **Don't wait for someone else to message you**. It's the year of our Lord, 2025. Regardless of your gender or sexuality, it's time to leave passive action at the door. Is it nice when someone else messages you first? Sure is. As women, we are socially conditioned to be sought after / on the receiving end of initiation. SCREW THAT. Shoot your shot. Take the risks. We're all just lonely (and horny) strangers scrolling on the internet. Let's cut to the chase and start reaching out.

5. **"I'm probably fatter in real life. If this bothers you, keep scrolling."** I read that line in a Buzzfeed article once about a woman who'd included it in her Tinder profile. It always stuck out to me as confident, brazen, and a great way to filter out people who'd have an issue with my body. As a plus-size babe in a world of suitors terrified of getting catfished, I used to swear by including this in my profile. But it was pointed out to me that a statement like that gives of a defensive, negative

vibe. I didn't want that. I wanted my profile to exude my
sunshiney, upbeat personality. Now I include a few
recent, accurate, full-body pictures. You know you've
been honest with your size, and if a date has a problem
with that—that's on them.

I say this acknowledging that including this disclaimer in my
profile was, in fact, the first thing my first ever date messaged me
about. In the wee hours on December 30th, 2022, I got a message
that started with, "I love how confident you come across. 'Fatter in
real life' you wrote? One, why should it matter? Two, even if it did
(which it doesn't) you just being how you come across is what made
me write you."

I was curled up in front of the hearth in my parent's kitchen,
doing the mind-numbing scroll of deciding if I was even attracted
to anyone, ever, at all …and that little bit of compassion went
further than any pickup line ever could.

I messaged him back.

Chapter 5

BRAVING THE DATING APP HELLSCAPE

I didn't know what to do in those first weeks of downloading the apps. Yes, I had made up my mind to be brave and to not quit, but I had no idea how those decisions would play out, or how quickly they would escalate. In accepting the personal challenge to go on dates before Easter, that meant *getting to know* and *connecting* with strangers. Gross. The thought of it made my introverted insides curdle. I wasn't looking for "true love" or a husband at this stage. I wasn't expecting to be arm-in-arm with a new beau by Easter. I just didn't want to be afraid anymore, and I wanted to accumulate as many romantic life experiences as possible.

I wanted to become a more authentic version of myself. I was tired of the psychological damage I'd done by holding in my pain and embarrassment over being a late bloomer for so many years. I tried talking to my mother in the past, but my reactions were always so visceral to her attempts to be supportive or comforting. Any time she tried to suggest that my experience was normal and that there was nothing wrong with me—that I was lucky, in fact, to have been able to experience life without heartbreak for so long—I shut her down.

She'd been happily married for 37 years. My parents had six

kids by the time they were my age and I hadn't even had my first kiss. How could she *possibly* know what I was feeling? Although I'd built a life I loved and had accomplished many things I was proud of, by the time I hit my thirties, the peace I'd cultivated around being chronically single had eroded. I would have traded any of my accomplishments for love.

Fast forward to my 32-year-old self sitting down with my mother and telling her that I was going to start trying to date, that I wasn't a teenager anymore (so I refused to sneak around), and that I had no intention of waiting for marriage to have sex. At the time, I'd lived at home, on my family's farm, my entire life. The big ol' house my nine siblings and I had grown up in had been divided up into apartments: one for my parents and youngest teenage sister, one for my grandmother, one for another of my sisters and her husband, and one for me. Although I knew we were in uncharted waters, I wanted to let my parents in on this new phase of my life.

By the end of my first week on the apps, I showed my mom the two guys who'd matched my conversational energy one night in early January. One was a teacher, the other a writer/former actor. "I'm talking to two guys right now. I kind of feel like a 'playa.'"

My mom laughed. "There's no ring on your finger, Allora, you're allowed to explore your options."

This conversation treaded new territory in a way that didn't make me wallow in self-pity or burst into tears. It felt like being included in a conversation I'd always wanted to be a part of, and I felt warmer, somehow.

She was curled up in the large, leather, green armchair beside a roaring fire in our old, brick hearth. I sat across from her, both of us in holiday pajamas with steaming cups of tea.

"They're both medium cute," I confessed, somewhat self-consciously.

She snorted. "Oh, don't do them that disservice. I'm sure they're both cute."

I pulled up their dating profiles and passed her my phone.

"Do you like one more than the other?" She scrolled through their pictures and prompts.

I shrugged. It had been almost two weeks of scrolling for hours, snap judgments on dating profiles, and making endless small talk. These two prospects stood out because they responded in full sentences, asked questions about my life, and answered questions about theirs. If you haven't braved the dating apps in a while, you'd be astonished how rare those kinds of interactions are.

"I think the teacher might ask me out soon," I told her. "If he does, I'd say yes. But the writer is taking his sweet time."

My mother sighed after a thorough profile perusal for both gentlemen. "No matter what," she said, "it sounds so exciting for you, Allora."

I couldn't get over how much that simple exchange meant to me. Neither of my parents had ever pressured me to date. In fact, my mother had frequently tried talking me out of the "there must be something wrong with me" melancholy I'd often slip into on the rare occasions I did express my emotions on the topic. In that moment of normalcy, a simple moment of talking about boys, I realized how much I'd always wanted that. It healed something; I just wasn't sure what.

The teacher took himself out of the running shortly after. Our conversation took an abruptly sexual turn that gave me the ick. It blew my mind how quickly I could connect with someone and just as quickly end it.

I wasn't ready to try starting up another conversation with someone else right away, but I continued talking to the writer. After two weeks, despite my prompting, he still hadn't asked me out. He told me he was starting a new career after pursuing his childhood dream hadn't panned out. Publishing a book and falling in love had been my two biggest dreams as long as I could remember. The thought of giving up on either one, and finding a new dream, struck me both as unbearably painful, but also incredibly brave. I admired that.

It sounds like you were really passionate about making your dreams work. Was it hard to leave them behind? I messaged.

I was out walking the perimeter of our farm after dark with my dog (a vain Pomsky named Digory), something I did before we settled in for the night. With all the snow, you could see pretty well in the dark. When my phone dinged, I pulled it out to read his reply.

That kind of intuitive empathy just earned you a date.

Someone had just asked me out on a date. I replied, *I wasn't looking for a prize, but that sounds like a pretty decent one.*

He proposed meeting at a nerdy burger bar, Swillburger, the following Saturday night.

I admitted, *In the spirit of honesty, I will tell you that I haven't dated much. I just never prioritized it. I was out building a life I love and dating is stressful/hard and the outcome is always uncertain. So I avoided it for ages, and now I'm out here winging all of this.*

It wasn't a lie and it wasn't the whole truth either, but it was as much truth as I was comfortable giving him.

Your dating experience is not an issue for me, he replied.

It was such a matter-of-fact response. He treated it like it was no big deal, and the conversation moved on. I *liked* that, that something I'd been ashamed of for so long could matter so little to someone else. We chatted a little more, but it was official: someone had asked me out. Hopefully, he wasn't someone who would stand me up or leave me hanging at the bar because, come hell or high water, I was going to Swillburger next Saturday night.

And I was terrified.

Chapter 6

SURVIVING SMALL TALK

Growing up, my father had all us kids read *The Fine Art of Small Talk* by Debra Fine. My parents wanted us to mature into well-rounded individuals. Learning how to talk to people was something they felt worthy of our time and attention. The point of Fine's book is that the easiest way to get people talking is to get them talking about themselves.

Some of those questions you ask can be poignant or practical, some might be silly. My siblings and I still jokingly ask each other, "How *do* you tell if a melon is ripe?" The point being, you can turn the smallest questions into whole conversations. Sounds great right? We grew up to be great conversationalists—the lot of us can talk to anyone about anything. You'd think this would apply beautifully to dating.

Well, yes and no. You can put all the energy you want into a conversation, but unless someone matches your efforts, all your small talk efforts will be for naught. When I expressed my frustration on TikTok, I was given a great piece of advice: "It's hard to maintain a conversation with someone you don't care about. So, learn about them, and care about them."

I present to you a list of questions inspired by TikTok to help survive the drudgery of small talk, along with my answers. I've printed out this list and keep it in my purse for dates. Even now, I'm always terrified of running out of things to say, and just knowing I have these always boosts my confidence.

1. Ask what they could give a 30-60 min presentation on, with no prep, that is not job related.
    - The travesty that was the *Game of Thrones* series finale and its lingering impact on pop culture.
2. What's your favorite kind of music/musician/song?
    - Elvis and Golden Oldies, all day long!
3. Do you wash your legs or just let the soapy water run down?
    - I stop at the knees. Keep your judgey looks to yourself.
4. What's your favorite part of the holidays?
    - The lingering and bittersweet joy of childhood nostalgia.
5. What's something you're looking forward to this year?
    - Any opportunity to go on a new adventure—big or small—is worth looking forward to!
6. What's the last belief you changed your mind about?
    - That racism has been eradicated in the US.
7. What's your most controversial belief or hot take?
    - Organized religion, when mixed with politics, can create unnecessary division.
8. What would your exes say if I asked about you?
    - Not yet applicable. Insert cringey winky face.
9. How do you handle conflict?
    - I try to empathize with how my actions, intentional or not, could have caused disappointment or hurt. My intentions might have been misunderstood, but that doesn't change the fact I caused pain, and I try to use that understanding to fuel a solution.
10. If you could take me on a date, what would we do?

- Anything involving movement—bowling, an arcade, mini-golfing, a museum. I like to be able to walk around when I'm nervous.

11. If you could do absolutely anything with your weekend, what would it be?
    - Visit somewhere I've never been or try something new, even within my hometown or a short drive away.

12. What do you do to take care of or improve yourself/quality of life?
    - Make sure I have device-free time on a daily basis.

13. Captions or no captions during movies?
    - You can pry captions from my cold, dead hands.

14. What were your favorite shows growing up?
    - *Batman the Animated Series*, *Lizzie McGuire*, *Arthur*.

15. What's the last TV show or movie series that you binged.
    - *Brooklyn 99*.

16. Is *Die Hard* [or any other film set during the holidays] a Christmas movie?
    - Absolutely yes and I will die on this hill.

17. How do you spend an ideal day?
    - Outdoors—can be reading, gardening, hiking, etc., but just out in the sunshine.

18. What's the last book you read?
    - *Legendborn*, by Tracey Deonn.

19. What's the last thing that made you cry?
    - Listening to the lyrics of "Beyond" by Leon Bridges.

20. What's something that made you smile recently?
    - An unexpected text that conveyed something sweet.

21. Ask to trade random facts back and forth for a few messages to spark more conversation.
    - Did you know that farm fresh chicken eggs can last for weeks/months on a shelf so long as you don't wash them first?

22. What's the worst date you've ever been on?
    - Too soon to tell at this point.

23. What's a movie you think everyone should see?
    - Iconic sci-fi films that start with "S" for sheer cultural significance alone.
24. What was your best/worst/weirdest trip?
    - My best/worst trip was my first international trip to Ireland with my best friend. I loved to stay in at night and read. She loved to go out and listen to music at pubs. We were so snippy with each other by the end of that trip—but we remember it fondly!
25. Where's the next place you'd like to visit?
    - New Zealand. Growing up with the deluge of early-2000s fantasy films being released did me in there.
26. What was your childhood dream job?
    - To be a jockey. It died when I got to be 5'9" by the time I was eleven.
27. What's your hype song? What song pulls you out of a bad mood?
    - Literally any song from the green ogre movie album (Millennials: you know what I mean).
28. Who is your best friend and how did you meet them?
    - I have two! The first saved me a seat once in grad school, and we've been besties ever since. She even officiated my sister's wedding. I met the other as models for a fashion photoshoot. Yes, really—I was paid! We taxied from the airport, met at a Macaroni Grill for dinner, and started immediately talking like we'd known each other forever. The rest is history.
29. Are aliens real?
    - The universe seems far too complex and vast for us to assume we're the only intelligent species within it.
30. What are your goals in life?
    - To live in a cottage by a stream, in the woods, with a giant draft horse whose forelock drapes over his eyes. To tell stories that connect people. To fall in love.
31. What's the most annoying thing a sibling has ever done to you?

- My childhood desk was next to the window in my bedroom. On a random Tuesday my little brother decided that everything on the desk belonged out that window. I had to pick out every beloved pen, notebook, and knick-knack out of the six-foot-tall hedges in the front of our house. He was not sorry.
32. What were you like in grade school?
     - A straight-laced people pleaser.
33. Do you have any interesting scars?
     - I have a scar on my chin. My younger sister cut the top of her thumb off with an apple peeler when we were kids. I was the lucky victim who was volun-told to hold a towel over it in the car as my dad frantically drove to the hospital. I passed out in the lobby the moment he disappeared around the corner with her, and woke up discovering that I needed to get about six stitches.

Chapter 7

WHO IS SHE?

How, exactly, does one get ready for their first *ever* first date? Because, only two weeks after "outing" myself as a late bloomer on the internet, here I was, trying to figure out what the hell to wear for the occasion. I knew how to dress confidently and what made me feel beautiful. What I'd never contemplated was how to style an outfit that represented me with the intention of looking attractive to someone else. Essentially…I was panicking.

When you think you're invisible, fashion choices feel easy. I had only ever dressed for myself. I'd told my therapist once that my invisibility was, in some ways, comforting. The fact that no one had ever taken notice of me romantically made it simpler to sail through life without the weight of perception.

She stopped me. "Why do you think you're invisible? You're here, and you deserve to take up space."

Well, damn. Sure. In all other areas of my life, I agreed. But dating meant convincing someone to see you, desire you, love you. And no one ever had.

The only thing I knew about my first date outfit with certainty, was that I would be wearing my favorite honeysuckle yellow pea coat (affectionately dubbed my "power" coat). There was *no* way my date could miss me in this yellow. I also settled upon black, skinny pants, a *dinosaur park disaster movie* graphic tee (gotta love copyrights), loose, white blouse, white sneakers, and topped off by my yellow power coat. It was me, somehow, even in its nerdy simplicity.

I poked my head into the living room where my parents and a few siblings were watching a movie. My mother and sisters (the best hype crew) gushed over my outfit and full-volume curls. My father, bemused, half-sternly told me, "Take a picture of him when you get there, tell him you're taking that picture, and then send it to me."

I kissed his cheek and promised to do just that. Was I excited? Absolutely. It felt like taking a first step I'd been waiting my whole life to take. I wasn't sure my nerves wouldn't kill me before I got there. My stomach twisted in the most godawful knots, worse than any nerves I'd ever had. It was snowing, and the roads were coated in thick, icy slush.

I scream-sang along to "I Have Confidence" from the *Sound of Music* on repeat for the thirty-minute drive, praying that my car would break down, that I'd get pulled over, or that literally *anything* would happen instead of this. I'd developed simple survival skills over the course of my life: avoid that which was scary, but also stave off disappointment by lowering expectations. Everything inside me was screaming that this act of bravery couldn't be as rewarding as curling up on my couch with a good book, or rewatching *New Girl*, or literally anything else. I was already operating under the assumption that the person I was meeting would either ghost me or that it would go poorly. That seemed safer than the alternative: that tonight could actually go well. Because …then what? What happened next if tonight *wasn't* a total failure?

I channeled my inner Julie Andrews and repeated over and over that *I could do this*. Even if this turned out to be the most horrendous date ever, I would be taking a step toward change, and maybe it would be less scary the next time I tried. I'd just switched over to Macklemore's "Thrift Shop" minutes away from the bar, slowing to a stop at the nearest traffic light, when I realized—with a jolt—that I saw him, my date: Grant.

It was a moment of slow-motion, like something out of a movie.

He was walking down the sidewalk, head bowed slightly against the snow, wearing a sherpa jacket, light denim, and thick-framed black glasses. It was all of a few-seconds glimpse, but it sank in that I was about to meet someone—a man. A man who had expressed interest in me. *Not invisible anymore*, I thought.

Fuck.

I pulled into the parking lot and sat for a minute with both hands gripping the steering wheel. I didn't actually *have* to do this. I could turn around right now, go back to my safe, quiet life, and live out the rest of my days in peaceful solitude. But I was done feeling like I had anything to hide or be ashamed of. I knew this was one more step in the direction of not being afraid anymore.

I took a deep breath and stepped out into the falling snow.

I tried to shove down my panic as I walked through the front door of the bar. We'd decided to meet here first for a quieter beginning and, besides the bartender, he was the only one inside.

Grant turned to face me, thick glasses gone. He had his own sense of style: simple but also refreshing. He wore a white Henley beneath his jacket and slightly fitted jeans over tan work boots. *Goddamn* was he ever tall.

I was 5'9", and although his profile said he was over 6', I hadn't anticipated what it would feel like, standing in front of a tall, handsome man as I tried not to gape. My chest tightened as he smiled and walked over to me.

"Hi! You're beautiful. Can I give you a hug?"

My cheeks flushed. "I—uh, is this the dating etiquette postpandemic?" I joked. "Is this what we do?"

"I'm okay with it if you are."

I smiled hesitantly and hugged him back, trying not to spontaneously combust at the contact. Try to imagine, if you will, my panic as I realized that I could barely string a sentence together. He'd asked me to be there, right? He was interested in me, or else he would not have asked. Every fear of rejection I'd ever had bubbled up inside of me. Surely, at any moment, he'd regret this choice. We'd just call it a day and part ways.

But he called me beautiful. He asked to give me a hug. He was asking me what I wanted to drink. We were actually *doing this*. I followed him over to the bar. I had a low tolerance and was picky about the taste of alcohol, so I didn't really drink. He ordered what was on special and didn't balk when that special turned out to be the manliest of drinks: a Mango White Claw. Somehow even that detail, too, made me smile.

After he insisted on paying for our drinks, I told him, "If we don't hate each other after today, it doesn't always have to be you paying."

He chuckled and we headed over to the nearest high-top table for a seat.

"I told my friends about you, you know." He popped open his drink. "About how much you love Elvis. They told me I had to watch the new *Elvis* movie—the Austin Butler one—before I came tonight."

I'd randomly, and obsessively, fallen in love with Elvis Presley the year before. Elvis merch dominated my wardrobe, my playlists, my movie choices, and I was wearing a TCB necklace. I beamed over this bit of intel, especially after adding that he watched it the night before with his mom, who'd been a big Elvis fan back in the day.

As far as I'm concerned, starting a date talking about Elvis is never a bad way to start. We dove into a lively round of small talk, starting with debating the accuracy of the *Elvis* movie. He asked me about my interests, how I got into Elvis, more about what I did for work. All of it was startingly easy. Conversation flowed organically. Although I was good at making conversation, I was something of an extroverted introvert. Nothing drained my social battery faster than having to solely carry a conversation, and it was one of things I was most worried about.

But this was not awkward. He asked me questions and answered questions of my own. We were both into a lot of the same fandoms, and the ones we differed on we were still able to have conversations about. He came across as secure in who he was and what he liked. Confident, but not arrogant. Chatty, but still giving space for me to express my own opinions. I paused us at one point before we got too deep in conversation. "Sorry, I promised my dad I would take a picture of you and send it to him. You know, internet safety."

Grant settled back on his barstool, leaning on his elbow as I blushed and took a quick picture.

"Should I be afraid of your dad?" he asked.

"Maybe," I said with a smirk as I sent the picture off. I was amazed that—at some point in the last half hour—my nerves had vanished.

"My dad is the kind of person who likes to take care of the people in his life. He is the one we rely on for, well, everything. The first person I call when something goes wrong. If we're travelling together, he's the first person I follow. He likes to, you know, walk into a room and take care of people, shake your hand, pay for the meal, that kind of thing."

"Oh, well, I'm kind of like that," my date replied.

My brows raised. *Am I into this?* Apparently, I was.

After about hours of fast-paced conversation, I realized I was starving and admitted as much. I'd been too nervous to eat all day. My appetite caught up with a vengeance. "It's already been two hours!" I announced as we finished our drinks. "Look how well we're dating!" The satisfaction I felt over the smallest of his smiles was undeniable. We headed for the door, which he held open for me.

"I hope you're not weirded out by old school chivalry," he said as I ducked past him.

"Oh no." My face flushed, maybe permanently at this point. "Not weird at all. Enjoying it, in fact."

The Allora that had been unleashed about twenty minutes into our conversation—I didn't know who she was. Charisma oozed out of my every pore. This Allora felt confident. She was cheeky, chipper, enthusiastic. Was I...actually having fun? Was I *flirting*?

We crossed the street and headed up the stairs into Swillburger. It was an old, renovated church that now hosted a burger bar and retro arcade. As we got in line to order, I was touching his arm for emphasis as I made jokes. A thrill tingled down my spine when I casually said his name. The arcade was jampacked with people and loud music. Once our food was done, we headed into a quieter room full of tables in the back.

We ordered the same thing—the house's burger special which was drenched in sauce and sauteed onions. There was no way to eat it gracefully. I laughed as we both made an attempt. It was the messiest thing either of us could have possibly ordered. We started talking and, again, it was startingly easy, how quickly time passed.

I took off my power coat as we ate, which spurred a whole conversation about epic movies and my love of both dinosaurs and dragons once he saw my *Jurassic Park* tee. I showed off some of my tattoos—including a massive Smaug tattoo lining my right forearm. Eventually we realized we were long past being done eating, and we should play some of the arcade games. He was funny, confident, and charming. I had not prepared for this scenario, and it was exciting to be enjoying myself while also having no idea what might happen.

Shocked? I sure as hell was.

He was a gamer and was at least vaguely familiar with most of the games. Mario on Super Nintendo and Nintendo64 was pretty much the extent of my gaming experience. We made it a point to look for some older games I might recognize. All the while, he never hovered over me or invaded my personal space as he showed me how to play each one. There was something so respectful about it that put me at ease.

So, what does this girl do?

This girl touched his arm, made sure our shoulders brushed when we stood side by side. When we played the seated *Jurassic Park* game (because obviously), I kept making sure our knees bumped. Just occasionally. Small, light touches that were setting my whole body on fire. How do I know how to do these things? *Who is she?* How did I know how to do *any* of this? I'd never flirted with anyone in my entire life.

Is that what this was?

I was stunned how easy it was to talk to him, have fun with him, laugh with him, to be near him. We finished up our gaming tokens. This date had lasted around four hours, and we decided to briefly head back over to the first bar to debrief. Karaoke was in full swing, so it wasn't quiet anymore. We huddled in the nearest corner, dipping our heads close to hear each other. This was the closest I'd ever been to a non-blood-related man.

I felt *alive*. Giddy—charged with electricity and heat. We were tucked away in the corner, outlined by the red neon signs in the windows beside us.

He asked, "How did tonight go for you? Be honest. Tell me. I can go first if you don't want to."

Beaming, I replied, "Honestly, I had a really good time. I had a lot of fun."

"Would you like to do this again sometime?"

I smiled. "*Yes*."

"Ok, good. Good. I think you're a really cool person, and we had a really good vibe together. I also had a great time, and I'd like to take you out again, if that's okay?"

I giggled, actually *giggled*. "Yes, I'd like that very much."

Again—who is she? I leaned in and gestured for him to bend his head closer so I could say something in his ear. "Can I tell you a secret?" I asked. Before he could answer, I blurted out in a rush, "This was my first ever first date."

I originally had no intention of telling him right away. Over messaging, all I'd said was that I didn't have much dating experience. It wasn't a lie, but not the whole truth either.

He smiled a little, glancing down at me. "I actually kind of got that vibe from you, but not in a bad way. You were just very direct and open with how you talked to me. It didn't feel like you were playing games, so it also didn't necessarily feel like you'd had a lot of experience. But it was actually really refreshing," he added before I could respond. "You have nothing to be embarrassed about."

"I'm not embarrassed," I shot back.

He offered to walk me to my car. It was still snowing pretty hard. We picked our way down sidewalks slick with icy pavement, talking as we did so. I had parked in a well-lit space and hadn't intended to let him walk me to my car. But his respect of my personal space had set me at ease. Despite all my not-so-subtle touches, he'd never touched me at all. It made me bolder.

I threw my arms out, gesturing towards my car once we reached my parking space. "She's all mine. Bought her with my grown-up girl money just last summer."

He smiled again, whether at my enthusiasm or at my outburst, I didn't know. "Can you let me know when you get home?" he asked. "I'll be in touch tomorrow. There's a Bills game on, so make sure you send the Bills your love."

I nodded, my face heating. I hardly noticed the chill or falling snow, even as he braced against the cold to talk to me. It hadn't occurred to me how this date would end until right this moment. I turned to face him, eyes wide and—hopefully—not too terrified.

"Can I give you a hug?" he asked.

I'd stressed about whether or not he was going to kiss me and if I'd have to explain that I'd never been kissed before. The relief I felt at this suggestion to hug instead was instantaneous. If he had initiated a kiss, I wouldn't have been mad. But it had taken every ounce of my bravery to show up that night. As he folded me into a hug, it felt right. He was going my speed and, intentional or not, it felt perfect.

It was everything I'd ever wanted.

He texted me before I got home. I had no idea what was supposed to happen next. I was not prepared for this possibility. I had only thought about a first date … not about what would happen if it went well and there were a second or third. I had only prepared for this date to go poorly.

It had not gone poorly.

Chapter 8

I'M A RAY OF FUCKING SUNSHINE

Now what?

Honestly, I thought there'd be more time before I had to prepare for this moment. Surely it couldn't be this simple. I had been prepared to go on multiple shitty dates with multiple lackluster people. I expected this process to be excruciating, boring, humbling, painful well before I went on a second date.

Now what?!

Grant texted me, as promised, over the next few days. We planned a second date for the following Saturday but—this time—I was tasked with choosing the place. I may not have had much dating experience, but *boy* did your girl have a decade's worth of potential date ideas. As we continued to message throughout the week, I was torn between liking this almost-stranger whilst simultaneously praying he wasn't a creep, rapist, or murderer. Fun times, right? We were barely connected at this point. Anything could happen. He could ghost me, decide this new connection was not for him, stand me up. There were so many unknowns.

I chose my favorite dessert place: Phillip's European in Rochester, NY. The last time I'd been there, they had this incredible brown butter brownie sundae and a Viennese meringue cake that was to die for. I figured, if it all went wrong or he didn't show, I'd still have dessert to show for it.

I sent him a handful of questions daily, which he answered and replied with a few questions of his own. I became invested. It is hard, after all, to care about a person you don't know. I wanted to know him and, I hoped, he wanted to know me, too.

I prompted him to share one picture, two songs, and three words to describe his previous year. His words, song, and picture told a story about overcoming heartbreak, pushing through fears, showing both vulnerability and hurt. It was such a small thing, those tidbits of honesty. But it felt like being invited to witness someone's soul, and I warmed to it. I shared my picture, two songs, and three words in turn with this strange burble of confidence I'd never quite felt before.

I texted him my one picture with a warning: *Please don't laugh. This was a power moment for me. I was hiking alone in Scotland and I'm sure I gave some poor old Scottish farmer a heart attack. But I decided to be a more honest version of myself last year, to do things even if they scared me, and to shatter any and all comfort zones. Hence this topless picture of me, from behind, on a mountaintop, in the Scottish Highlands.*

He texted the next day, *I had a therapy session today and you were the bulk of the conversation as it turned out. She asked me if I noticed any red flags. I told her, "She may have a warrant in Scotland for indecent exposure."*

I snorted. Excitement thrummed in my veins. Mind you, it

might not be the most revealing picture in the world, but I had sent a *topless* photo to a *whole ass man*.

Who *is* she?

He did not make me feel weird about what I had shared, and—even more—had made me laugh out loud. Also, gotta love a man in therapy. *Chef's kiss.*

After finding out *Wednesday* was on both of our watch lists, he suggested we start watching it so we'd have a bonus topic of conversation for our next date. I loved the idea.

I may be more than you bargained for, I told him. *That could be a red flag.*

Confessing my late bloomer status had loosened something inside of me. I never wanted to hide a secret ever again, and I was determined to word vomit every thought that came to my head. The harder a thing was to say, the more determined I was to share it.

Just don't be a pessimist, he replied. *I've had my fill.*

I'm an insufferable optimist, I warned. *Be careful what you wish for. Someone who's constantly in search of a silver lining.*

As we continued our conversation about vulnerability and baring all—literally and figuratively—something else had started to bother me. My videos documenting my fledging dating journey had continued to get more and more popular on TikTok. In just three weeks, I'd accumulated thousands of followers and hundreds of thousands of views. I had no life experience as an "influencer" on such a public platform, but not telling him about my TikToks was eating me alive.

I spewed it all in another texted confession. First and foremost, I wanted him to know everything I'd said was genuine, and I that was *not* using him for content. Second, I explained why I was making the videos in the first place (accountability, community, "shedding shame" as a late bloomer, etc.). To my eternal horror, I concluded by sending him links to my first date recap and told him how much continuing to share this journey meant to me. The 30-minute wait for his texted reply felt like the longest of my life.

I mean this in a kind and playful way, as that was very brave of you to admit. Has just every guy you've ever met just literally punched you in the face or something? If I'm the nicest guy you've met, I'm dying to know what shit luck you've had to meet what sounds like the jerkiest of jerks before me.

His levity felt like a sign or, at the very least, an instant tension diffuser. Here I was, with *another* confession, and he was—again—treating it like it was no big deal. My relief was immense and overwhelming.

I was a late bloomer, too, Grant continued. *I met someone who was an even later bloomer than I was. It taught me a lot and helped me grow into someone more experienced and wiser. Like Yoda.*

The worry that had been gnawing at me from the moment we met dissolved through such simple conversation. Good lord! What an oddity it was to be laughing over secrets I'd held onto for *so* long.

I'm literally blown away and so MAD that I spent so many years being embarrassed about it. Like, UGH, I AM A FUCKING RAY OF SUNSHINE. And the only one dousing it has been me. Anyway, please don't sell yourself short, sir. You are EXTREMELY nice, very cool, and very much worth getting to know. Talk to you soon … and thank you.

Confession time ended, for now. We proceeded as planned for our next date that weekend.

Was I nervous as hell driving up to meet him? *Abso-fucking-lutely.* My playlist had absolutely zero chill. We went from listening to Elvis' "Such A Night," to "Make Me Know It" to "Fever" (all flirty songs) in quick succession. Between the King and my impending date, I was capital "F" flustered.

Phillip's European looks a little like the height of its grandeur was in the 80s, with faded pastels, antique floral booths, and a heavily mirrored bar. The lighting is always dim, which only adds to its unassuming charm. I'd only ever been to this dessert place during weeknights with friends because we liked avoiding crowds. Grant was already at the bar. I didn't know, until then, that I was into gentlemen wearing thickly knitted, open-front cardigans.

He walked right up to me, gave me a hug, and apologized, "We're not going to be able to get a table. We didn't make a reservation. But we can sit here at the bar." He gestured to the stools behind him.

My face flushed. "Shoot, I should have thought of that. Is it okay if we at least stay for dessert and then go somewhere else for dinner? They have *really good* desserts."

I hadn't been there in over a year because I was on a bit of a health journey. I was still on said health journey, but there's always time for a little bit of cake. I appreciated that this was not a big deal. We were quick on our feet and handled it positively. I ordered tea, he ordered a drink, and we took a walk to the brightly lit dessert case to browse the mouth-watering selections.

I pointed out which one was my all-time favorite—the Viennese meringue cake (a strawberry shortcake hybrid accented with a sugar cookie crust and crisp, white meringue).

"Well, we definitely need to try that one." His voice was deep. He stood beside me, hunched slightly to peer at each dessert in turn. This was *wild* wasn't it? Insane even? That I would be standing shoulder to shoulder so nonchalantly with a whole ass man. After all my years of solitude, this felt like an impossibility.

He chose a classic salted caramel cheesecake.

"I approve," I told him with unfamiliar cheekiness. I leaned towards him, smiling. "Now I get to try it, too."

The oddity of this familiarity was not lost on me. I wasn't sure who this new version of Allora was. This Allora knew when to laugh and when to smile, how to lean towards said date, and who'd just invited herself to sample an almost-stranger's dessert. *Who is she?*

Dessert selected, we sat at the bar where our drinks waited. I made myself a cup of Earl Grey tea with milk and a splash of honey. We made appropriate Piccard jokes and joked about *Star Trek*. Such a happy pair of nerds. I raised my teacup without thinking. "Cheers." I waited until he clinked my cup with his own. When our treats arrived, I proffered my unused fork. "Cheers." I grinned. His answering grin delighted me as he tapped his fork against mine.

"You have to try mine first," I told him seriously. The hefty slice of cake, in all its strawberry meringue glory, falls completely apart under any kind of pressure. "While it's still beautiful and together."

"I'll trust you on that." His fork lifted as I slid it over to him.

My heart pounded, but my overall panic started to subside at these signs of familiarity. Even if it was all pretend, something was working. I was acting like we'd known each other forever.

He offered me the first bite of his cheesecake.

"Good," I assured him, "but not as good as mine." Again, conversation was lively, with a natural rhythm of questions and answers on both our parts. This second date lacked the sharp energy of the unknown that tinged our first, but the warmth of that familiarity mixed with burgeoning hope was uniquely calming. Without admitting it, we both clearly wanted to be here and were curious about where this might lead.

Desserts finished, we walked across the street to a medium-fancy Italian place for our backup date location. We got seated right away in a crescent-shaped booth and slid in on either end, maroon cushions cracking beneath us, meeting in the middle. I faced him, knees forward. It was louder in here, so we scooted closer to be heard over the murmur of conversation.

For someone who is a notorious overthinker, I was settling into the feeling that this date was going well. He had a sort of calming presence that was difficult to explain. I'd been nervous walking through the door of the first restaurant, but the moment he folded me into a hug, the tone of the evening felt more like catching up with a good friend than going on your second ever date.

We started getting into some deeper stuff. If our "safe zone" was talking about hobbies and the fandoms, this time we started diving into more personal things: joys, fears, wins, losses, heartbreak. Sometimes it can be hard to say a real thing, even to people you've known and loved your whole life. And it is hard to share those beginning tendrils of emotional intimacy with someone you barely know. I could feel us being careful, tiptoeing around this tentative connection. We were still sort of strangers, but—in this moment— we were trying to be more. We eventually got dinner—something cheesy and smothered in sauce for me and, of course, my trusty lemonade. I could not get over how comfortable and chill it all felt. As someone who'd lived in terror of dating, I couldn't express how special that was for me.

One of the conversations we'd had prior to this date was about the speed with which I needed to move with him and dating in general. I told him I appreciated him being patient and open because I was fighting to overcome my internalized fear and anxiety. Having someone not pressure me in any way and being open about going at my pace was freeing. I was not embarrassed to have those boundaries set, especially around sex and physical intimacy. How he responded to them was comforting. It took the edge off my worry. As the date came to an end, I surprised myself when I realized I was sad.

As we crossed the parking lot back to our cars, passing streetlight after streetlight, I got nervous again. We hadn't said anything about what happens next. Clearly, there was something good happening, but we hadn't addressed it head on. *Now what?*

We were still chatting and walking, walking, *walking* until my heart felt like it might explode. I stopped and grabbed his arm.

"Listen, I'm sure we were gonna talk about this sometime, but I'm having a really nice time with you …and I'd like to see you again." I said, my heart a wild, frantic thing. For the first time that night, I couldn't meet his eyes. I was churning with butterflies. Was he having a good time, too? Would I see any inkling of hope in his answering expression? *Was this it?*

My relief intensified as, silhouetted by streetlights, he laughed. "Of course, I was going to talk to you about this. Can I finish walking you to your car first?"

"I know, I mean yes. I just—" The words stuck in my throat.

"*Allora,*" he said firmly, gently.

I realized I was still holding his arm, and I released him like I'd been burned. My breath hitched at the sound of my name.

"It's okay. I'm having a really good time, too. I would also like to see you again."

Apparently not satisfied with my current level of word-vomiting, I continued, "I just wanted you to know that I was talking to other people, but I'm not now. I—I just want to see where this leads." It still felt difficult to look him full in the face, but I did.

Something like amusement tugged at the corners of his mouth.

"I'd also like to see where this leads. I'm also not talking to other people."

Hope surged within me. My face felt like it was on fire. We crossed the street, pausing beside my car.

Before I'd gotten there that night, he had texted me a heads up. *I don't want to startle you. I know you've said you're 'skittish,' but if our date goes well tonight, I'd love to give you a kiss on the cheek. If that's ok?*

I alternated between "touch is terrifying" and "I would love *more* than a kiss on the cheek." The phrasing and timing were considerate of my comfort level. As our breath misted in the cool, night air, I tensed, waiting for something—a sign that indicated, yes, this date had gone well and that he was—in fact—going to kiss my cheek.

I unlocked my car, tossed my leftovers on the passenger seat, and turned around to face him.

Before I could say anything, he said, "I think tonight went really well, and we can hash out the details for date three later. But can I give you a kiss on the cheek?"

Why an anticipated kiss on the cheek suddenly felt daunting—I had no idea. I asked in a small voice, "Is it okay if we hug first?"

He opened his arms, and I melted into him. I slid my arms inside his open jacket, tucking my nose into the hallow below his jaw, as he wrapped broad arms around me in a firm, warm embrace. I'm Italian, and one of the ways the women in my family greet is with a quick lip brush on the cheek. I gave him one of those and pulled away.

He chuckled, tapping his cheek with one finger. "I think you can do better than that." Still absolutely aflame, I collected my nerve and stood on tiptoe, planting a proper kiss on his cheek before I could think better of it. My lips brushed the neatly trimmed stubble peppering his jawline. When I pulled back, he waited a beat.

"My turn." His answering kiss was light and gentle, but that beard stubble might as well have electrocuted me. My entire body felt like a live wire.

Biting my lip, I took a step back towards my open car door—astonished by how not scared I was.

"Text me when you get home, okay? Let me know you made it?" he said.

I asked for another hug. We embraced and I slid into my car.

He watched me drive away, waving when I pulled out of the parking lot and onto the road. I smiled the whole way home. I had no idea where this was heading, or what I even wanted, but I knew that I liked what was happening. I liked how it felt. No one was more surprised than me when, just three days later, I invited him over for dinner.

Who the hell is she?

Chapter 9

CAN I HAVE ALL THE KISSES?

My childhood home is an old farmhouse, nestled in the Genesee valley, that's plenty big enough for ten kids to romp around. Since we'd all grown up, that house had been broken up into apartments: two were standalone and two shared common living space. I lived in the latter part, sharing space with my parents. The other two apartments were taken up by other family members. My parents were, *mercifully*, not around for my date night. I'd invited Grant over for dinner so that we could finish *Wednesday* together. My goals for the evening?

One: I wanted to show this gentleman my life. I had an unconventional living arrangement, but it made a little more sense when you saw it.

Two: I wanted to be kissed.

I texted him the day before because, despite my hesitancy around dating, I didn't want to be treated as a delicate, broken thing. *You know, please don't treat me any differently. Be normal around me. Yes, I am skittish, but if something is too fast or too much for me, I will be very vocal about it.*

He replied, *I hate to break this to you, but I have been treating you normal this whole time. But if you're giving me the green light to make moves on you …*

don't worry about it. I got you, girl. He also asked what my favorite movie candies were so he could bring snacks.

My plan was to cook dinner, cuddle, watch *Wednesday*, and then? Well. We'd see where the night led.

By the time he walked through the door, dinner was ready, and I'd been pacing for the 20-odd minutes that he'd been late. We exchanged hellos and gave each other a brief, warm hug—an instant tension diffuser, before he peeled off his jacket. My dog, Digory, decided to come over to investigate. Digory was a territorial little shit, but also the actual love of my life. When my poor date reached out to pet him, Digory responded with an *absolutely not, no thank you*, jerking his head back and snapping his teeth.

I shooed him from the room, mortified. "He's really shy."

Grant shrugged. "Don't worry about it. He'll get to know me."

My brows raised. *Oh, will he now?* I gestured for him to sit at the island countertop across from me while I plated dinner.

He set a sack of candy, drinks, and popcorn down beside him.

"The chicken is overcooked." I flipped quesadillas over in the pan, giving each a quick reheat.

"It smells delicious, I'm sure I'll love it anyway."

"It's weird," I tell him, "I've never cooked for a gentleman caller before."

He smirked a little, rolling up the sleeves of his white Henley. "Is that what I am? A gentleman caller?"

I flushed, smiling as I slid him his plate. "Yes, that's what you are." As promised, he ate every drop of my overcooked quesadillas.

After dinner, I gave him a tour of the farm. Even though it was dark and had snowed recently, you could still see fairly well on a clear night. We bundled up Digory—still wary but more polite—who followed us out and trudged out into the crisp night air.

"This is my whole life," I explained, "taking care of the farm. In the winter it's slower because there's less to do outside—which is a nice break. But the rest of the year is pretty busy for me maintaining the property." Taking care of the house, the yard, the animals: it consumed the majority of my time outside of work.

"That sounds sort of relaxing, in a way, though," he replied.

Feeling surprised by my own cheekiness, I replied, "Well that's good, because there'll be plenty for you to help with around here come spring."

We fed my chickens, looped around the pond at the top of a small, sloping hill, and headed for our riding arena. I was bundled up in a warm, winter jacket. Grant was not. His sherpa jacket did not look warm enough, although he didn't complain as we stopped at the edge of the arena. It was the highest point of our farm. The surrounding forests, fields, and farms stretched out before us in an undulating wave that went on for miles. On clear nights, it felt like standing inside the sky. It was too cloudy to see stars, but we still had a beautiful view.

"This is my favorite spot." I turned to face him. We huddled together against the chill, shoulders almost brushing, but he was making no moves. Zero moves. Despite my hopes for romantic opportunity, I realized this man was too polite to tell me he was freezing. In momentary defeat, I suggested we head back inside.

I gave him a tour of the main parts of the house. He loved my living space (obviously, as I have excellent taste). I beamed at his praise. Eventually, we grabbed our spiked drinks, Sour Patch, and popcorn and moved into the living room.

There was a big, navy sectional in one corner, with framed posters of my family's favorite movies lining the walls. We positioned ourselves on either side of the sectional corner to turn on *Wednesday*. I had predetermined that the corner of the sectional would be ideal for cuddling.

"Sit in this spot." I pointed. "It has the best view of … the TV."

Your girl is nothing if not strategic.

Without batting an eye, he did, but how he angled himself meant that there was no subtle way to scoot up to him without it being obvious that I wanted to cuddle. I didn't want to look desperate, or like I was coming on too strong. I didn't have a suave bone in my body. Zero rizz. Instead, I sat as close as I could without being super obvious and hoped for the best. We turned the lights off, and the episode began.

Although we were sharing a bowl of popcorn, I promise you, no two people in the world have ever been so careful not to touch hands while fishing out dainty popcorn servings. We kept pausing to let each other get a handful before going in for one of our own—the waiting hand hovering awkwardly. We were comfy, munching away, *not* touching, while we watched this show. We even chatted a little, something he apologized for.

"Sorry—I don't always talk when I watch things. I just really love movies."

I shook my head. "It's nice. Like an extension of our date." We weren't just sitting there in silence. I liked the ebb and flow of the conversation. As we finished the penultimate episode and began the finale, I couldn't help but feel like my date was being a little … distant?

We sat there, chatting away and having a good time, but *no moves were being made.* He hadn't so much as glanced my way once the episode began. He was fully concentrating on this show. Which, I mean, fair. Jenna Ortega was killing it. But I wondered, *Do I even like this guy? Am I enjoying this? Yes, I am enjoying this, but I don't just want a new friend to nerd out with. That's not the vibe. Mama wants some suga. She's been waiting her whole life.* I couldn't tell what the issue was. We'd been having a nice time, conversation had been light and lively, and I'd been clear about giving him the "green light," hadn't I? Were we literally going to "Netflix and Chill" *without* the chill?

I was working on being more forthright, but there was only so much bravery a skittish, late bloomer could expend at once. It wasn't, by any means, a bad date, but nothing was happening.

I wanted more.

It was nearly 11 p.m. by the time *Wednesday* ended. We both had work in the morning. He turned to me, not quite meeting my gaze, and asked, "Should I … go? It's late."

I blinked, smiling encouragingly. It hadn't occurred to me, until this exact moment, that maybe he was also nervous. "I mean," I responded with mock seriousness, "we're already up past our bedtimes. I think we can make an exception. "

He nodded, finally looking up at me. The soft glow from the TV silhouetted his face. "Then I have sort of an awkward question for you." He reached for the remote. "And I'm going to put some music on to cut the tension."

Despite my nerves, all I could think was: *kiss me*.

"Trust me." He flipped through some ambiance videos on YouTube before settling on a soft jazzy library. "It helps."

I was sitting cross-legged across from him, a jaunty sort of expression on my face as I waited. There was something endearing about it all: his nerves, the preparation, the question I was hoping he'd ask. I felt alive, like electricity had been swapped for the blood in my veins. I was humming with it.

"You've never had dating experience before, right? We've talked about that."

Amused, I nodded. "I've been in an unrequited love situation that broke my heart and took me years to get over, but no. Nothing besides that."

"So, you've never been kissed?"

Blushing, I shook my head.

"So, two things," he began slowly, like he was bracing to say something hard. "Just trust me on this, when you kiss someone for the first time, you form a kind of link with them. You remember it forever. And I don't want this to be a bad or painful memory for you if we don't work out. I don't want that for you."

At first, I did not like the direction this rant was going. Was he *lecturing* me about wanting to kiss him right now? I was grown up. I knew what I wanted even if I wasn't amazing at articulating it yet. He started to ramble, clearly flustered, as it started to dawn on me what he was trying to say. He was warning me that this was a memory I'd have forever, and did I want to have that memory *with him?*

"Are you afraid of wrecking me?" I asked. "Is that it?"

Visibly relieved, he nodded. "After my last relationship, I feel like I've only just put myself back together."

I warmed to this vulnerable truth. "So you're scared, too," I said, my voice soft.

He frowned. "I'm not scared of you."

I gestured between us. "You're scared of being open to … whatever this is. We're wary of each other, and we're coming at this having experienced heartbreak on very different ends of the spectrum, but it's still there. We're wary of it."

"Yes, exactly."

"Well, I think—to quote my mother—it's unwise to borrow worry. I don't think it's a good idea to go into something expecting it to fail. But, knowing that it can, we can't promise not to wreck each other. But we can promise to be honest, and we can promise not to disappear. If things aren't going well, we can talk about it and end things amicably. We can be adults about this." I raised my hand with my pinky finger extended. "Pinky promise?"

He studied my face for so long that I wasn't sure he'd take it, but then he raised his own hand and curled his pinky around mine.

He met my eyes. "Can I kiss you?"

My newfound charm and bravery evaporated. Poof. Despite the whole speech I'd just given, my stomach dropped. "Yes—of course yes," I said, continuing on in a nervous babble, "but I don't know what I'm doing. Just so we're clear, I've never done this before—"

Kissing is terrifying as a late bloomer. You understand the logistics, but you feel too old to not fully comprehend technique, or how this could possibly be pleasurable when you've never put your mouth on someone else's before. In general, I'd never been as physically close to anyone's face as I was in that moment. I was a fish out of water. When you're faced with the kind of panic that only another human can help you overcome, it is a humbling, petrifying experience. You are at your most vulnerable, most raw, all while combatting years of embarrassment that you haven't crossed this bridge already. You are an adult, but you feel childish.

He pursed his lips, which caught my full attention. "Well, do you want a funny first kiss or, like, a romantic first kiss?"

In a giddy rush I replied, "Well can we do a 'take one and take two?' I want them all. I want *all* the kisses."

Holding back a smile, he scooted closer. "Then let's rip off the band-aid first. We'll do a quick peck."

He was sitting in front of me. No one had ever looked at me with this kind of intent before. I leaned in and—in a moment of pure panic—I pulled back and blurted, "Do I go left? Do you go right? How do we—"

He shook his head. "Don't worry about it," he said, his voice low, soothing. "Just a quick kiss." I leaned back in and, for the briefest of moments, pressed my lips against his. I yanked back, my face heating.

"Are you alright?" he asked, bemused as I grinned and brushed my fingertips over my lips.

"I'm fine," I managed, breathless.

"We're going to try again. I'm going to put my hand in your hair, alright? And don't pull away so quickly this time. Try and stay there a little longer."

Eyes wide, I nodded. "Okay."

He leaned forward, his finger tangling in my curls, and gently kissed me again.

That proximity and contact was simultaneously exhilarating and the most awkward thing in the whole world. Teeth weren't hitting and noses weren't bumping, but still … is this what a kiss is? *Am I kissing?*

"Are you okay?" he asked when we broke, our faces inches apart.

I was trying to be brave, and I did feel comfortable around him. He was being careful with me, but I was still scared. I didn't know if I was doing this right. I didn't know how to become less awkward. I was looking forward to more practice, but I couldn't seem to squelch my panic. For the second time, as we pulled apart, he joked about something that I can no longer remember, but it made me laugh.

He nodded. "You've just had your first funny kiss. You laughed. Now you can kiss me any way you want."

I froze. Because, *uh—sir?* I didn't know how to do that. I didn't know how to do *anything*. We were still sitting on the couch facing each other. It felt juvenile. After a moment's contemplation, I stood up, took his hands in my own, and pulled him up. *Oh my God*, I realized, *there's a whole grown ass man in front of me.* My eyes widened as I looked up at him. "*Oh*," I said softly.

"I know," he said, almost apologetically, "I'm tall."

To be clear, I didn't *mind*. It was just intimidating.

"You're fine though," he encouraged. "You're doing great."

I nodded, biting my lip. Momentarily overwhelmed, I pitched forward and gave him a hug. He wrapped his arms around me without question. A persistent thrum vibrated through me. The sensation wanted to explode out of the center of my chest. I was not uncomfortable, but I was terrified.

I want to tell you that I was concentrating on the magic of this moment, but all I could think was, *I don't want to mess this up.* Gathering my courage, I looked back up at him, his face still highlighted by the soft glow from the TV, silly jazz music playing in the background.

The way he looked at me was unbearably sweet, soft, tender— like he cared about nothing else, in this moment, other than making this special for me.

"You ready to try again?" he asked.

I blew out a breath. "Okay."

"This time," he said, "I want you to put your hands here." He guided my hands to his hips, pressing them into his side. I didn't have a single clue where my hands had been all this time. "I'm going to put my hands around your waist," he continued as the weight of them settled. I looked up at him, closed my eyes, and I leaned in to kiss him again.

He was not aggressive or forceful. His mouth was soft beneath mine. He was asking, not taking. It felt like he knew what he was doing, even if I didn't, and I was just trying to stay there, trying not to let my overthinking drown me.

Am I doing a bad job? Is this a bad kiss?

I didn't know. I started to tremble. I was shaking, actually shaking. He must have felt it, too, because we pulled apart, the heat and weight of his hands around me like an anchor. He didn't let go. Instead, I caught my breath. I don't know who moved first, but our foreheads pressed together—just for a moment.

"You know, you're doing great," he repeated. "Are you okay?"

I was not *exactly* freaking out, but I was actively trying to calm down and, as we stood there, I was calming down. I was still shaking —a tremble that spread down my shoulders and arms. "Yes," I responded, annoyed with myself. "I just feel like I'm bad at this." A beat. "Am I bad at this?"

"Don't worry about it," he replied. "You're doing great."

"You're just saying that to be nice, aren't you? You don't have to be nice—"

"*Allora*," he cut off my babbling. "I don't just say things to be nice."

I was speechless, gazing up at him.

"Would you like to try one more time?"

I paused, took a deep breath, and nodded.

The last kiss was the longest. I stayed in that moment as long as I could, focusing on the novel sensation of his lips gently parting mine, his stubble against my chin, the weight of his hands—one snaking up to tangle in my hair, my body pressed against his. It was the single most romantic thing that had ever happened to me. I would love to tell you it still wasn't awkward, but it was.

All I could think was an endless loop of: *Am I doing it wrong? Am I opening my mouth enough? Do I have too much spit? Are my lips too stiff?* I couldn't seem to siphon off the litany of worry harassing my brain. He took it all in stride though, remaining patient, reassuring, and sweet.

Despite all the ways I had thought about my first kiss going wrong, I'd never contemplated it going so sweetly, brilliantly right. When we broke apart, we rested our foreheads together one more time. I laughed softly and threw my arms around him in a tight hug.

When I released him, still in the tangle of his arms, he was smiling. "You're blushing. It's really cute."

I snorted. "I mean, *yeah*." The lights had been dim. He must not have noticed the consistent blush that had been creeping up my face the whole night.

"Are you 'all atingle'?" he teased. "Oh wait—sorry. That sounded more sexual than I meant it to be."

I chuckled amazed, still holding onto him. "No, it's fine. I am … 'a tingle.'"

"Are you okay?" he asked. When I nodded, he continued, "Then how about we wind down from this moment?"

We sat back on the couch and watched a few episodes of *Harley Quinn*—but this time, your girl made a beeline right for his side. I looped my arm through his, no invitation required, and laid my head on his shoulder. He leaned his head against mine. We snuggled up: legs flush against each other.

He sighed. "You have really nice hair."

"Thank you," I replied. "It's my pride and joy."

We sat, cuddled up together, for another hour. It was perfect, and it was now 1:30 a.m. We needed to be up in a few hours for work. He got up, collected his things, pulled on his coat and shoes.

"When are you coming back from your trip?" he asked once we were out by our cars.

I'd told him earlier that I was going to San Francisco for work that weekend, and I'd be gone for eight days. I loved travel, but the timing of this trip just as my first *ever* romance began felt less than ideal. He promised that we'd talk while I was away and figure out our next date.

Once I was back in bed, I cried for a full five minutes, just over the sweetness of it all. I'd never envisioned what a first kiss could look like for me. As I got older, that daydream grew increasingly painful and, thus, one to avoid. It had seemed inevitable that a first kiss for my late blooming self would be embarrassing or awful. There was no way it would be beautiful or something I'd never forget.

But the way he looked at me? How considerate and encouraging he'd been? How he did his absolute best to make it feel like it was all normal and fine, that we were even having a good time? I'd had the time of my life, and even though we ended on a good note, I didn't know what we were now. We'd pinky promised to do our best not to hurt each other, but what was that? Was that dating? Was that a relationship?

I texted him before I went to sleep:

I literally cannot thank you enough for these sweet 'firsts' you are giving me. To quote Wednesday Adams: 'You are leaving an indelible mark.' We can't promise not to hurt each other, we just can't. We're both wary of heartbreak, of being hurt again. And we're looking for safety, and safety is also something that's hard to promise. But you have already shown me that you are very considerate of making me feel safe. I don't know how to make you feel the same way. But I can promise to be loyal. I can promise to be compassionate. I can promise not to ever ghost you. I know we're both wary of getting into something serious, but I am serious about seeing where this goes. Do you want to try?

As far as I was concerned, I hadn't started this dating journey intending to jump into a serious relationship straight out the gate. I planned on being a player and going on multiple (probably bad) dates. I hadn't expected to get into a relationship with someone within three weeks. I wouldn't have held it against him if he wanted to back out. I didn't even know if *I* was ready for this. I hadn't expected to be in a position to want to try. But I didn't feel like being afraid of something not working out was a good enough reason to not try.

He replied that afternoon, *I'm sorry I took so long to reply. You send pensive messages late at night sometimes, and it takes me a minute to figure out what I want to say.*

That was true and partly strategic on my part. When I told him about my lack of dating experience, my TikToks, and now this—all said revelations had been late at night so I could go to sleep, not stress about it, and get a response later the next day.

He continued, *I don't know why you're so insecure about this. I understand why you are—but you don't have anything to be insecure about. The way you handle yourself checks every emotional fulfillment box I could possibly have. I was already there last night, but yes—I would like to give this a try. When you come back, would you like to meet my parents? My mom really wants to have you over for dinner.*

Chapter 10

KISSING ADVICE

One of the most intimidating things as a late bloomer is anything having to do with physical intimacy, especially kissing. When I've admitted this, I've had people ask, "But didn't you just practice on your hand or your pillow?" or "Haven't you watched movies?"

Sure, I had, but *none* of that actually helped. I still felt like I was approaching something kids learned how to do in grade school. I am a firm believer that you can learn something new at any age, but kissing was different. My fears around it were potent, consuming, and mortifying. There is NO way to practice ahead of time without involving another person.

Do you feel my terror?

If you haven't had your first kiss yet, and you're just as terrified about it as I was, know that I know where you are coming from. As someone brand new to the game (and *very* much enjoying herself), I've compiled a few tips. From one overthinker to another, I hope some of these help.

I wish you all the kisses. xoxo

- **Tip #1**: Don't give your kiss away to someone you are not comfortable being around. This kiss on the first/second/third date rule? Fuck it all. If you are not ready to kiss somebody—don't kiss them. Alternatively, if you are feeling good about kissing someone, kiss them!

- **Tip #2**: Relax—I know. Worst advice *ever*. I got in my head about kissing. A persistent thrum of, "Am I bad at this? Am I awful? Am I doing this right?" It was a cyclone of worry that made an already vulnerable moment more intimidating. Someone suggested I have a glass of wine or a mildly trippy treat to curb my nerves. I can say from experience, a teeny glass of wine *did not* hurt at all and did loosen me up a bit. If imbibing is not your thing, try going for a walk before your date/kiss, or something to burn off some of your nervous energy.

- **Tip #3**: Breathe through your nose when you're kissing, not through your mouth, so you're not blowing your mouth air into theirs.

- **Tip #4**: Relax your lips. Unclench your jaw. Think about your mouth being soft.

- **Tip #5**: You don't need to lick your lips. Wet kisses get sloppy. Alternatively, it's hard kissing with chapped lips! Treat yourself to some lip balm ahead of time if needed.

- **Tip #6**: For first kisses, leave your/their tongue alone. Save that exploration for when you're feeling braver/more confident. Kissing is still fun without tongues being involved.

- **Tip #7**: The movement of kissing is similar to taking the top off a soft-serve ice cream cone, or the icing off a cupcake, with your lips. All lips—no teeth, no tongue. It's a simple, soft movement and not an extremely large bite.

- **Tip #8**: Close your eyes once your face is close enough to know where you're going.

- **Tip #9**: I'm a huge fan of letting your … kissee? … know that you're new at this ahead of time. Odds are, they can help you through it. And if they can't, that's a red flag, babe!

- **Tip #10**: Not sure what to do with your hands? When in doubt, they can rest on your partner's forearms, shoulders, waist, or hips. You can also cup their head with your hand. Think "high five," with their ear in the space between your thumb and fingers. Or, my personal favorite, sink your fingers into their hair at the nape of their neck.

- **Tip #11**: Start small, like a five to ten second peck. Then try a longer one. Stay in the moment, mimic that ice cream/icing motion for a little longer. You'll loosen up and unwind before you know it.

- **Tip #12**: When you're feeling braver, depending on when you're sitting or standing, let your hands run down their side, arms, down their back, or through their hair. Simple, intentional, and slow movements can be hot.

- **Tip #13**: Don't lunge forward to start. Approach and start slowly.

- **Tip #14**: Kissing doesn't have to stay at the lips! Explore the chin, cheek, forehead, neck with your kisses. Neck kisses are glorious.

- **Tip #15**: Remember, everyone had to learn how to kiss. It's something you can learn, learn to do well, and genuinely have fun doing it in a short amount of time.

- **Tip #16:** Be kind to yourself! Bodies can be sloppy and messy and kissing is no different. Don't beat yourself up if it doesn't go perfectly the first time. Practicing is good fun.

- **Tip #17**: Go slow. Don't aim for a steamy make out at first. Aim for a series of slow, sweet kisses—one after another—until you get the hang of it and are feeling more confident.

- **Tip #18**: If you are thinking too much or, alternatively, having a great time—feel free to sigh. It relaxes your brain, and it lets your partner know you're having a great time.

Chapter 11

UNREQUITED LOVE

Leaving to go on a work trip—and for over a week at that—felt like the biggest cosmic joke ever to a newly-kissed late bloomer. I'd just been KISSED. People might get kissed every day, but I was thirty-two years old. I'd been dreaming of a first kiss for as long as I could remember. It had almost been a full month since we'd started talking, and we'd both agreed that we wanted to see where this led. Why, only a day later, did I find myself panicking again as I started packing for my trip?

This man knew what I looked like, what my life was like, what my dating history had been, how nervous I was. He'd been unfazed by it all. In some ways it felt easy, this connection, but my brain kept popping up with new ways to worry me about it. *All this*, it hissed, *could be a lie*. Or something would pop up to make my gentleman caller understand the error of his ways in being attracted to me at all. The future seemed dangerously full of hope and suddenly wide open in ways I'd never anticipated.

Everything impossible felt within reach. It tantalized me. So why, *why*, as I meticulously overpacked, did I find myself crying and drafting explanations as to why Grant should steer clear of me?

Because although all of this was starting to feel a little like magic, I'd had a taste of magic before. And being so wrong about that past connection had taken me years to get over. It had made me question everything I thought I knew about myself. Seven years later, here it was, haunting me again.

One month after finishing my first semester as an actual teacher, I realized that I *hated* teaching. Just like that, it felt like my graduate degree had not only been expensive, but also a gigantic waste of time. All those years of college had never once prepared me for the possibility that I would end up hating the career path I'd been working toward for a quarter of my life. After a profound month of "Oh *fuck*, what now?" I ended up working as a bank teller for $10.50 an hour. Although I was grateful to have found a job that allowed me to quit waitressing, I felt unmoored. I knew I hadn't completely wasted my time by getting my degrees. I would pivot, find a new path. But, right then, it all felt a little … pointless, like I was starting over.

I took to being a bank teller quickly. I was friendly and handling money was oddly satisfying. It was a straightforward job and a welcome change of pace. Shortly after I started, we hired another teller to fill the spot next to mine. He was handsome, tall, sharply dressed, with a sarcastic sense of humor that—despite my best efforts to remain aloof—won me over. He was the sort of person who liked everyone around him to be happy. I was 23, a size 18, and between being plus-size and my late bloomer status, I was convinced I was invisible. I had a healthy dose of self-esteem, and I loved how I looked regardless of my size—but I also knew I was not *objectively* pretty. We didn't match. I decided the moment I met him that he was too handsome to notice me and, although I was never mean, there was no way we would ever be friends. I wasn't worried about "catching feelings" for him because I knew he'd never truly see me.

For some reason, my new work buddy took my initially polite, but frosty, demeanor as a personal challenge to win me over. What started as competitions to see who could answer the phones the fastest and grabbing lunch together escalated to full out prank wars. I once arrived hours early just to tinfoil his *entire* workstation and fill several of the drawers with Hot Cheetos—his favorite. We laughed so hard on our shifts together that our manager had to reprimand or separate us. We started to hang out after work.

It wasn't until our work Christmas Party months later, when we took a group photo while I was standing beside him, that I realized I had crossed a line. I didn't see him as a coworker or a friend; I *liked* him. I cropped that team photo into an image of just the two of us, pulling it up when I was alone and imagining what dating him would look like, feel like, taste like. It was the first time I'd truly envisioned myself being with someone else. We exchanged numbers and started talking all the time about things I'd never talked about with anyone else, let alone with a *man*. A *handsome* man.

He invited me over one night after work. I offered to make dinner (fajitas, my signature dish). His housemate wasn't home. I'll never forget sitting across from him at his tiny, white kitchen table. The house was fairly neat for two guys in their twenties. He was from out of state but had come to New York to stay with his best friend from college and to volunteer at his local church. He was a gifted vocalist and musician, and deeply connected to his faith. He was lonely out here, away from everything he'd ever known. Somehow, him admitting something so personal—that loneliness, how he'd struggled getting used to living here—made me comfortable being vulnerable too. I knew something about loneliness.

"I've never even been on a date," I told him, cheeks flushing as I admitted this for the first time to a *whole ass man*.

He'd shrugged mid-bite, unbothered, hitting me with that warm, bright smile. "Not anymore. This can be a date."

I don't remember a thing he said after that, because that single sentence was stuck on repeat in my brain. I wondered if I'd misheard him. I must have misheard him, right? There was no way that's what he was saying. There was no way he might actually like me, too … right? We'd become close, and I knew that we'd crossed into actual friend territory. We had inside jokes, texted constantly, ate lunch together almost every day, attended different events together outside of work. But he was objectively gorgeous. Everyone liked him. I'd watched customers bring their single granddaughters into the bank just to introduce them when they made their deposits.

I knew, generally speaking, people liked me, too. But not like that. Never like *you are a beautiful thing, and it's criminal if someone is not in possession of you.* I was likeable because I was friendly, but I was also fat. No one, as far as I knew, had ever looked at me twice.

Despite all of that, the fact that he was stunning, and I was not, had started to matter less. He had seen me when no one else had. We became best friends. He met my family. We invited each other over for holidays. In the spring, when he asked if I wanted to be his accountability partner at the gym and do a crazy clean diet with him—I said yes. Neither of us had admitted to having any kind of romantic feelings, but losing some weight couldn't hurt. I committed to our plan with feverish intensity. I lost 60lbs and four pants sizes in three months. I worked out twice a day, cut out carbs, sugar, caffeine, alcohol, and red meat. It was exhilarating. I finally had a body that I thought could be worthy of him.

Some of the older women at the bank would tease that we were an adorable couple. Gorgeous. "You'd make the most beautiful babies," one told me.

Me … *gorgeous*? I'd never thought of myself that way. I ate up the validation of other people seeing compatibility between us, too. It all felt golden. Bright. Exciting. And he was so much fun. I had no idea I could be so comfortable around a man I wasn't related to.

"There's something I want to tell you," I said one night, leaning against my parked car, arms folded over my chest.

He was across from me leaning against his, both of us haloed by the harsh glow of the overhead streetlight. "Oh?" A smile played on his full lips.

"Yeah, but I'm not sure … it might change things between us."

"Well, you *have* to tell me now."

Even though I initiated this conversation, I felt myself stalling. It felt childish to admit this out loud, despite how close we'd become in the short time we'd known each other. "I like you. Like, *really* like you." I instantly wished I could take it back even though that admission had exploded out of me.

His blank reaction stretched into an excruciatingly awkward pause.

I panicked, said goodbye, and left.

Later that night, I cried, embarrassed, and took shots of Fireball Whiskey with my best friend. I texted him an apology, saying that I didn't want to make things weird.

"There were plenty of signs that he's into you," she reassured me.

There had been signs, hadn't there? I'd gone over them all in detail, analyzing every intimate conversation, every late night, every lunch date. We'd talked about our dreams, our futures, our pasts, challenging each other's long-held beliefs from different ends of the organized religion spectrum. We'd talked about our families, our hopes, our fears. This was a connection, the likes of which I'd known with my closest friends, but never before with a man or with an element of physical attraction. It held a different weight.

Don't worry about it, he eventually texted back. *You didn't do anything wrong.* Nothing else.

I was devastated. I didn't go into work the next day. I felt like, despite all that we'd shared, I'd broken some unspoken rule. I'd crossed a line I hadn't realized existed, and I didn't know how to uncross it.

Come back to work, he texted. *Everything is fine.*

It should have been the end of my hopes right there. Because he hadn't said yes or no, all my heart had heard was, "maybe." I let that ambiguity fuel my dreams.

I wanted to transform myself into whatever he wanted. I started to pay more attention to the styles he appreciated: simple, classic. I stopped wearing brightly colored or funky print dresses and patterned infinity scarves, trading them for stripes and neutrals. I grew out my pixie cut, a staple style for me through grad school, because he told me once he preferred women with long hair. I stopped defending myself when he'd poke fun at the things I liked, like superhero movies or fantasy epics. I fanatically worked out, tracking everything I ate.

Because, maybe then, his hesitation—whatever it was that was preventing him from liking me back—would cease. I could transform that non-answer into a yes.

From the moment I met him, I'd known there was a deadline to our time together. He'd only been planning on staying in New York for a year or so. Despite the fact he'd been talking about moving back to the West Coast for months, it still felt like a gut punch when summer came and those plans became reality. We went out one night shortly before he left. He'd brought his best friend, I'd brought mine, to try out a local Mexican place in Rochester. We ordered drinks and pounded crisp tortilla chips, fresh salsa, and street tacos.

My bestie offered to drive so, on this rare occasion, I allowed myself to let my hair down and drink. We both wore new dresses for the occasion: she in bright coral and me in a retro mint number that accentuated our summer tans. The boys dressed in short-sleeve polos and fitted slacks. The lighting was dim, the drink refills frequent. The alcohol and good company took the edge off everything.

Eventually, we decided to head out. We were on the second floor of the building, and our friends headed down the stairs in front of us. He was far drunker than I, and he stumbled a bit when he rose from his chair. I watched him wobble as he tried to straighten.

Laughing, I slipped beside him and slid my arm beneath his shoulder. "Come on big guy, I've got you."

We followed our friends, but he stopped me, swaying. He looked down at me, his gaze unfocused, grinning widely. "Kiss me."

My expression slackened. The haze from my drinks temporarily cleared. I distinctly remember my panic as I pulled away, eyes wide, searching his face. "*What?*" I must have misheard him. After months of saying nothing about my initial confession, now he was *what*?

He swayed again, gripping the handrail. "Kiss me."

I swallowed hard. I'd wanted nothing more for over a year and, at the same time, nothing less. He knew how I felt. He knew about my lack of experience. He knew what this would feel like for me. My cheeks heated. The dim glow and noise felt suffocating.

"I—I can't," I stammered. Did I want to kiss him? Absolutely. Did I want a kiss, my first kiss, to be here? Now? A drunken exchange in the middle of a packed restaurant? I turned away, feeling small, as heat expanded from my chest down my shoulders, my face, my ears. "We should follow them."

He didn't protest as I gestured for him to walk ahead of me, my hand hovering above him to stop him from falling. It had happened in all of a few seconds. Our friends, still breezily chatting away, hadn't even noticed our delay. They opened the front door as we both made it to the landing, walking ahead of us towards the parking lot.

Before he could round the front of the building, I caught his hand. Adrenaline burned through me. He turned back, brown eyes unfocused. I looked into his face. "Did you mean what you said back there? That you wanted me to kiss you?"

He nodded lazily, absolutely fucking plastered.

"I don't know how—" I stammered. Petrified. "I've never—I need you to show me how."

He studied me a moment, my eyes pleading.

His friend called after us to catch up, diverting his attention.

My heart hammered as he turned away, wordlessly, to follow after them.

Too late. *Too late.*

Too scared.

I had ruined it. I should have just—what? *Thrown* myself at him? Nothing about any of it had been like the fantasies I'd nurtured. But no one—most especially him—had ever asked me such a thing before now. What if I never had another opportunity?

It was a long drive back to the house the boys shared. Our friends, still having a lively conversation, slid into the front seats. Someone turned some music on. I sat beside him in the back, at first furious, embarrassed, forcing a smile. As my mortification abated, the alcohol haze slammed back into me. Hard. I forgot to be hesitant, or ashamed, or fearful. I thought of nothing as my head felt too heavy to hold up, and I leaned against his shoulder. My foundation stained his sleeve. I let my head fall into his lap when the dizziness didn't go away.

The back of my head nested across his thighs. I looked up at him, studying the curve of his jaw, his thick, black hair. He rested an arm across my waist, igniting something brazen inside of me. I reached up, hesitantly, running my fingers through his hair. He let his head fall back against the seat and sighed. I traced circles on his bicep, the crook of his elbow, his forearm. Without a thought in the world, I slipped my fingers beneath the hem of his shirt and traced the ridges of his abs—fingertips stroking up and down each bump, finding the plane of his chest.

It was as though all of my inhibition had floated away, emboldened by the drinks and the requested kiss. He breathed deeply. I had never been in proximity to someone like this, had never touched anyone with this kind of intent. I marveled at how my worries vanished.

I rolled over onto my side, facing forward. My shoulder pressed into his hip. I looked down to make sure my dress was smoothed out.

The metallic clink of his belt buckle jingled.

Confused, I looked back and saw him fumbling with his belt to unzip his slacks.

Without warning, his other hand gripped the back of my head and pressed toward his crotch. I was unsure what either motion had to do with the other.

He pressed on the back of my head again.

I froze, understanding what he wanted.

I pushed myself upright. Oddly, I didn't feel panicked, only sad. I slid my fingers over the hand still fumbling with his pants, stilling the movement.

"No," I said softly. "Not like this."

A glassiness coated his eyes as he looked back at me.

"You don't want this," I told him.

"I do," he mumbled.

I shook my head. "*We* don't want this. We'd hate each other tomorrow if we did this."

I don't know why I felt so calm, why I trusted so implicitly that he'd listen. Although I wanted nothing more than to be wanted by him, and to make him happy, a blowjob in the back of my best friend's car was *not* what I wanted.

Spell broken, he relaxed again. He released his hold on his belt, hands drifting to his sides. I laid my head down back in his lap, oddly unbothered. Foolishly unafraid.

We fell asleep like that till we made it back home.

We dropped the boys off and, wide awake, I filled my bestie in on what had happened. We were excited at first, but that morphed into outrage.

"So … what? He'll ask for kisses and blowjobs, but can't admit that he has feelings for you?"

She was right of course. It was ludicrous.

I'd made plans to go kayaking with him the next day. I knew we'd have plenty of time to talk about it then. It was hard not to be wild with the hope of it all.

It's happening, finally happening, I'd thought. This had to change something. It must.

I still had no idea why, after months of entangling our lives with deepening friendship, he'd still never given any sign of wanting something more. But that night had proven something … hadn't it?

The next morning, I picked him up with twin kayaks in tow. We set out down the river, him quiet and nursing a hangover, me waiting for some explanation, some acknowledgement, and feeling increasingly confused as none came. When I worked up the courage to ask, he admitted he'd been too drunk and didn't remember any of it. He was sorry.

Neither of us said a word the whole way back.

He moved back home by the end of the summer. That should have been the end of it. I was devastated. I didn't understand how he could just say goodbye.

"Maybe we can see each other once or twice a year," he told me.

How could "once or twice a year" be enough for him? Why wasn't it enough for me? I stood, one cloudy afternoon, by the fence line on our farm. My mother leaned on the fence boards at my side. I cried my eyes out, telling her everything, telling her I'd follow him across the country if he asked.

"I know you love him, Allora. Because, even now, you're trying to figure out what you would sacrifice to make this work." She paused, her tone softening. "But I don't think he loves you."

Days later, when my dad asked me about it, he tried to say the same thing. "Love shouldn't be this hard, sweetie."

I wanted to believe they both were right, but my parents were high school sweethearts. I was 24. What did they know of living a life alone? Of the shame I'd carried over being perpetually unseen and unchosen? How could I explain that, no, it shouldn't be this hard. But it should also count for *something*, shouldn't it? Could I really have gotten this close to someone, connected this deeply to another person, for it to just not matter at all now?

I couldn't accept it.

You'll eat anything if you've been starving long enough.

WE STAYED in touch like he'd never left. The long text conversations continued. I'd take his calls at midnight, 1 a.m., 2 a.m. —I didn't care about the time difference. Neither did he, apparently.

I scored tickets to my first-ever Comic-Con in San Diego the following summer. I was thrilled at the prospect of seeing him. It was like no time had passed. We picked up right where we left off with all of our inside jokes and favorite stories. We blasted all of our favorite songs. I stayed in California for two weeks, one with one of my sisters where we vibed and thrived in all our nerd glory at Comic-Con. The second, after my sister flew home, I spent with him at his parents' house. It was my first time meeting his family. His mother took me shopping. I went to dinner with his sisters. I was the thinnest I had ever been, and he showed off my "before and after" photos, bragging how he'd been the best personal trainer.

I met his cousins, aunts, uncles, and his niece. After too many drinks one night, I pulled one of his sisters aside for advice. Did she know what I was doing wrong? If he'd ever said anything about liking me?

She shook her head. "My brother is complicated, but you can't force love. He'd make it happen if it's what he wanted." She said it kindly, but it didn't lessen the sting, or my hopeful delusions.

On the last day, we drove to another family member's house, killing time before heading to the airport. "You don't know how miserable I've been," I said. "How much I've missed you. How hard it's been without you."

"*Allora*, I can't be your only source of happiness." His tone was unexpected, sharp. He had never been angry with me before. Tears burned in my eyes before I could stop them.

"I'll just take an Uber," I replied.

He sighed. "Don't be silly. You're staying with me till it's time to go."

I didn't understand it, how he could still be so happy. Our impending parting felt like doomsday. During a lull at his sister's house, we fell asleep—side by side—on the couch, arms folded over our chests in an accidental, mirrored post. His mother took our picture and sent it to me, commenting that "it was so sweet that we were such good friends."

Another year went by, and I still couldn't seem to shake my feelings. Our conversations stalled, but picked up speed as the holidays came round. *I can do this*, I thought. *I can just be friends with him*. I had accepted we were never going to be more, but I didn't believe it until we started talking about dating other people.

I downloaded a dating app and sent him pictures of the one guy I'd started talking to.

"He's not good enough for you," he said.

I snorted. "And you're the best judge of who is best for me?"

"Of course. We're best friends." He never expressed emotion like that, and it took me aback. Despite the unexpected warmth at his protectiveness, nothing could have prepared me for the moment he sent me a picture of a girl he'd started to see. They'd met for coffee for a first date. She also spoke Spanish, went to his church, was also musically gifted. They shared tons of interests. It all made sense. Surprisingly, none of it stung until I saw her.

"Send me her picture," I told him, proud of myself for how

supportive I was being. I was healed, see? I could be a good friend. "Let me be the best judge for *you*, buddy."

She looked small standing beside him. She was deeply bronzed, with long, dark hair, petite. The top of her head barely came to his shoulders. It had always been a deep-seated fear of mine that I was, simply, just not his type. You can't force physical attraction, and he'd never given me any indication of being physically attracted to me.

It had always stung a little, but never so much as in the moment when I realized how wrong everything about me was. I was too tall, too broad, too different, still too fat. I was not enough and too much at the same time. He never loved me because I'd never been what he wanted. In an instant, everything we had been felt like a lie. My body felt alien, wrong, and like it had failed me.

That didn't stop me from staying in touch or visiting three more times over the course of the next year—once for Comic-Con again, once for a work trip, and once for Dia de Los Muertos. We went out during Comic-Con, got plastered, and came back to my Airbnb. Knowing he didn't want me didn't stop my flash of pleasure when a stranger told us we were a smartly dressed couple—even when he explained we weren't together. It didn't stop me from curling up into his side, sleeping with my head on his chest all night.

His mom took me out shopping again. She bought me a purse and asked me if I had any idea what her son was struggling with. She was worried about his partying, or why he'd stopped singing at church. She felt like he had a problem, but she didn't know how to help him. I should have been more worried about him, but instead I was delighted that she asked. It meant that other people saw I was special to him, too. Even though I should have recognized how little I was willing to accept, it felt good to matter to someone. To him.

These breadcrumbs were more than I'd ever had. I cherished every indication of our continued "closeness," every intimate detail that we shared.

I cried every time I flew home.

.   .   .

I DIDN'T KNOW it would be the last time that I saw him. He paid for half of my plane ticket to visit in October. I flew out on Halloween. I visited with his family again, who were all as warm and welcoming as ever. We went out that first night alone for drinks.

I sat beside him in a booth in downtown San Diego with a massive margarita each. We caught up on our lives—we'd been talking less at this point. Despite the fact that he'd never admitted to any romantic feelings for me, I couldn't let go. It felt like proof that we were something special. See: this *wasn't* just a crush. Unrequited love, maybe. But the inherent tragedy of unrequited love felt like it gave my feelings some realness. Tangibility. *See*—I'd tell myself—*this is something real.*

He turned to me, the weight of his full attention wholly arresting. "I'm sorry for putting you through this for all these years. You deserve so much better. I'm so sorry for treating you this way."

The apology was so heartfelt, so unlike him, so out of nowhere that I didn't know what to say. The warmth of it lit me up. I *mattered.* He was *sorry.* He knew, despite my loyalty, that he'd been toying, unintentionally or not, with my emotions.

He *knew* it.

The streets were crowded when we left and, knowing how anxious I could be in crowds, he reached back for me without looking, took my hand and guided me through. I would have followed him anywhere.

I was giddy the next day. We were going across the border into Mexico to spend the rest of the weekend in Tijuana with one of his friends. Even though I was certain that something would never happen between us, it didn't stop the most brutal flare of hope from igniting within me once again.

That night I wore a skin-tight black dress, did my hair up in an elegant twist, and stained my lips with a "fuck me" shade of red. I almost never wore lip color. I was too self-conscious of how big it made my lips look. Not that night. I wanted to have fun, to look fine, and—most importantly—to be *seen.* With some unprecedented confidence, I wanted to show him what he was missing. We went to a quieter bar for drinks first. The three of us laughed, took shots, caught up, got to know each other. I loved getting to know his friend: he was sweet, considerate, funny. A 10/10 kind of human.

We migrated to the bar next door, with its outdoor terrace, for dancing. It was dark. Strobe lights and strings of twinkling bistro lights illuminated the bar. We were just friends, I knew that. But all it took was one dance to break me.

The three of us stood around a high-top table, nursing brightly colored, sweet drinks as the music swirled around us. He grinned at me, gorgeous, confident, and offered me his hand. He knew I hated dancing. I didn't have a drop of rhythm in my entire body, but he shook his head at my panicked refusal.

"Come on, I'll show you." He took both my hands, leading us out onto the dance floor and pulling me in close, twirling me.

I feel like people can forget the intimacy in touch alone. I don't know if it was the close proximity or because the alcohol caught up to me, but grief hit me like a tidal wave. How could we be this happy together and not *be* together? I didn't understand. I never understood. And here I was, visiting him again for the third time this year, and for what? Was I okay with all of this? What was so profoundly unlovable about me that he never wanted me?

I held back tears as he guided me across the dance floor, the strobe lights flitting across our skin. He guided me forward, back, our heads bent, his expression soft in the cool blue light. I didn't start crying until I made it back to the table while he used the restroom.

"What's wrong?" His friend asked, placing a hand on my back with genuine concern. I didn't mean to be so honest, but my misery was a gaping wound. I couldn't seem to staunch the bleeding.

"I *love* him," I choked out, covering my face with my hands. This person barely knew me, but he pulled me into a hug.

"He needs to talk to you," his friend said quietly.

I don't remember why the friend temporarily left, or how I ended up back at the bar, snotty and miserable, ordering another drink. That's where he found me. I leaned against the bar, facing the dance floor, drink in hand, swiping away my streaming mascara.

He stood beside me, crossing his arms over his chest. "You've been crying."

I didn't answer. I took a long sip of my drink, watching the few people still dancing.

"Do you want to talk about it?" he leaned closer to be heard above the noise.

Fuck. It *hurt* that he thought he had a right to know anything. He had *made* me into this broken, bruised, pathetic thing. Worse, I had allowed it. I'd happily become someone who hung on his every word, happy to snatch up breadcrumbs of affection hidden within texts, late-night calls, visits, and heart-to-heart conversations for *three fucking years*. Three years I'd wasted loving him, hoping for him, figuring out who I needed to be for him, what I needed to sacrifice in order to make "us" work.

I looked at him, really looked at him. My jaw tightened. "Are you gay?" It was sharper than I meant it to be, but I was desperate for some explanation as to why I could love a person so much, and for them to just not love me back. After a lifetime of being alone, it all felt cruel.

"No." His smile faded.

It was the first time I realized that loving a person could maybe hurt worse than hating them. My love for him was an agony for us both—a burden he felt such guilt over, and a heaviness I couldn't seem to release us from.

He got drunker—so drunk that his friend and I had to help him stand, each of us beneath one of his shoulders. We led him out of the bar, onto the street, heading back to the hotel room the three of us had split. He stumbled at one point, and I caught him, held him up, and then he was hugging me tightly and … crying?

I was so confused by the sudden outburst of emotion. His embrace. His tears. I didn't stop him as he slid to the curb, his face in his hands. I don't remember where his friend went. Maybe he just hung back a few steps to give us a moment alone.

"Allora, I've begged God to make me love you. You're perfect. But I just … don't. I see how it's hurting you."

It was the most tragic thing I'd ever heard. There was some

relief, too, in the admission. He recognized, too, that there was something unique between us, something special. A connection neither of us had experienced before. He admitted he hadn't wanted to be clearer about his feelings (or lack thereof) because he hadn't wanted to lose me as a friend. Which, if I thought about it clearly enough, meant that he'd put his own needs above my own. Even though he'd seen me hurting, he'd still chosen what was better for him.

A reasonable part of me knew that was fucked up, but the louder part of me reverberated with the fear that I hadn't been enough. I couldn't help but wonder: what would ever be enough?

I still kept in touch for months. Listening to him talk about dating, making suggestions for what to get his dates for gifts, where they could go. I boxed away the part of me that cared. In my own way, I wanted to be a good friend.

He asked me to help him update his resume, but he'd forgotten to mention he also needed a cover letter the next day. I had work deadlines of my own going on that night that prevented me from writing said cover letter. He'd been annoyed.

It wasn't until then that I questioned why I was beating myself up over this. Why was I still jumping through hoops for someone who, again, prioritized his own needs over my own? *Why* had I continued to allow this?

I cut ties. In the end, it was that small argument that woke me up.

We didn't speak again for years. When he reached out to apologize for leading me on, for taking advantage of our friendship, to ask for my forgiveness, I did not allow myself to rekindle the connection. I forgave him. I bore him no ill will, but I also told him I never wanted to speak with him again. If I changed my mind, I'd let him know.

I mourned that relationship for *years*, the bits of good from our friendship itself, the time wasted, the emotional investment. It broke something intrinsic within me, shattering any trust I had in myself. How was I the kind of person who would choose someone so wrong for me, someone who'd never loved me, over and over again? If I could be so wrong, *for so long,* how could I trust my own instincts? Could I trust anyone, most especially myself? I clearly had no common sense, no better judgment. And—worse—as the years marched on and I continued to go unnoticed and unloved, it solidified my certainty that I was, in fact, unlovable—a grotesque thing perpetually undeserving of a romantic partner.

That, coupled with my own embarrassment over my lack of experience, ate me alive.

I wouldn't find myself making videos to do something to change my own perception or shed my shame for another seven years.

Then I met Grant. Then I'd kissed Grant. Not two days later, desperate to explain a burgeoning explosion of physical insecurities, I sent him another "pensive" late night text.

Chapter 12

RUNAWAY TRAIN

Are you attracted to me?

That was how I opened a text to Grant the night before I left for San Francisco. Even though what had happened with my unrequited love situation hadn't actively haunted me in several years, it was making me second-guess everything. Every insecurity, every lifelong fear I'd carried of somehow being abhorrent or invisible, it all came crashing back. Despite the fact that I'd always been plus-sized, going through various weight loss and regain cycles through my twenties, I'd built up a healthy dose of self-esteem around my physical appearance. I believed I was beautiful in every size, but my self-perception felt irrelevant as I wondered if I was attractive, specifically to him. After all, I'd been emotionally connected to a man before, and I'd been wrong about everything.

I don't mean 'do you think I'm pretty', I continued. *I'm aware that I am glorious. But are you, in fact, attracted to me? That kiss was not, in fact, a pity kiss, and this is something real … isn't it?*

Every new confession felt like picking at wounds long since scabbed over. I couldn't shed these insecurities fast enough. I wanted to word vomit them all out and scare him away before I got in any deeper. In the texts that followed, I told him everything about that unrequited love. Or, at least, the most important bits—that I'd given my heart to someone who never loved me in the same way, that I spent years heartbroken, wondering what about me had been so wrong, and that, most importantly, as a late bloomer, I didn't really know what being on the receiving end of attention felt like. I thought I'd known, but I'd been wrong before.

I don't know if I trust my own instincts.

I fell sleep crying into my pillow, certain that I'd sabotaged something that had felt promising, all because I couldn't rein in my own emotions. They felt like they were spilling over a dam I'd built over a lifetime, and I didn't know how to stem the overflow. As I waited to board my flight early the next morning, I received a response:

Allora, if I was not attracted to you, I wouldn't have pursued you after our first date. I think you are very pretty, and have found a fantastic way to channel your insecurities into something much more positive and helpful (TikTok). We can second-guess all we want, but the truth is our pasts are behind us. Both of us recognize a good thing is happening. I, for one, refuse to let the sins of someone else who wronged me in the past, no matter how good they were, sabotage my happiness any further. I do not know much about us yet as a 'unit,' but I do know that we seem to bring out the best in each other, and seem to have the answers we both have been missing for what has felt like long enough. Don't let that voice in your head convince you otherwise.

I blubbered through takeoff, flooded with relief at sharing yet another fear and being met, once again, with understanding. It felt like a balm mingled with excitement. It was the joy of discovering a connection with a kindred spirit. That person, in turn, was looking for that same connection with me. It was terrifying in the best way possible, but also wildly and unexpectedly good.

Flying fuck, I texted back. *Is this how you expected your year to kick off? It's really taken me aback.*

In the grand scheme of things, a week is not a long length of time. But now that I had someone I wanted to kiss again, it felt like the longest week of my life. I'd gotten good at travelling alone over the years. I'd brought books to entertain myself. I had a list of places to visit and restaurants to try. I'd even made plans to meet a new online friend in-person that I'd met through a shared love of Elvis. Normally, I would have been delighted by any opportunity to travel, especially when my job was footing the bill, but it also felt like waiting for the next episode of a show to come out after a "to be continued" fade to black.

I *wanted* to be continued. Badly. By all means, *continue me*.

We sent each other a video message—another first. I replayed his over and over, for months. I sent him pictures of my colorful, professional outfits for each day of the tradeshow I was working. We scheduled our first phone call for early in the week.

When I told my mother how nervous I was, she said, "It's insane to me that your generation doesn't talk on the phone more."

Even though we'd been in consistent communication for about a month, those conversations had been primarily through text. I paced in my hotel room a full half hour before he called. I stared at the screen until his contact picture popped up—the one I'd taken during our first date.

Would it look too eager if I answered on the first ring? We were both adults. Did stuff like that even matter? To play it safe, I answered after three.

"Howdy stranger," I said.

"Hello," he replied, his voice calm, deep, and still unknown despite our increasing familiarity. The conversation flowed from there. Twenty minutes went by. Thirty. We talked about my trip, what I'd done so far and what I was planning to do tomorrow. We talked about California and climate change, favorite movies, whether or not we wanted kids. An hour flew by. I was astonished by both the length of time and just how easy it was to talk to him.

There were no lulls or awkward silences. He matched my energy, asking me questions. I spent the tail end of that conversation curled up on my side of the hotel bed, facing my phone lying on the pillow beside me. I beamed once the call ended and we both said goodnight.

I shared, along the way, my thoughts and fears around dating on TikTok. Only a month into documenting my dating journey, many people congratulated me which, despite the sweetness, confused me.

It seemed like the internet thought I had strolled into my very own "happily ever after." But, at the end of the day, I was winging this. Should I be feeling a sense of accomplishment here? I mostly felt a general terror—and maybe a little like I was losing my mind.

The thought of seeing Grant again made me nervous. But when I was with him, I was becoming more happy, content, and comfortable. I knew that he would text me every time around the same time and we'd have a lovely conversation. Every day, I couldn't help but wonder, is this the day he doesn't text? Is this the day it all ends? Is this the day he realizes he's had enough of me?

I didn't know. I'd never been in this situation. I felt like I was being pulled in all these emotional directions, between joy and terror, fear and hope, and, occasionally, the depths of sadness as I explained my past, my loneliness, and as I tried to not assume the worst would happen. All emotions felt like extremes. There was no middle ground. I'd always been someone who was content doing her own thing, spending my time any way I chose. But knowing that I had all these days to myself, I should have been pleased as punch to read books or write every night. Instead, I stared at my phone for hours.

Is this what dating was? Is this what it felt like? Everyone kept telling me to "enjoy the ride," but this ride felt like driving down a bumpy road when you really have to pee—the dread of knowing what could go wrong felt smothering. It didn't matter if people told me not to overthink or stress. I couldn't turn off my worry.

There was so much hope inside of me, wrapped up in it all—the certainty that this could end at any moment but also the persistent thrum of possibility. Yes, it could end, but what if it didn't? What if it kept going?

What if?

The weekend after I got home, I went to meet Grant's parents. My nerves waned each time I saw him. This time, I was nervous, but in the same way you were nervous for a job interview or to go to the doctor's: normal nerves, not "fish out of water" nerves. I wasn't afraid of being around him, I was just nervous about making a good impression.

I stopped on my way to get his mom flowers and felt cute as hell in the outfit that I'd picked (a green dress with white polka dots, black tights, and pointed, white, ankle boots beneath my yellow "power" coat). His parents had invited us over for dinner. I pulled up, knocked on the door, and heard their dog bark from inside. By the time the dog was crated and Grant opened the door, I was grinning widely.

He had a single yellow rose in his hand.

I had a wildflower bouquet in mine. I held my flowers out. "Oh, obviously these are for you. Just kidding, they're for your mom."

He smiled. Ahead of time, he'd suggested that we get into the habit of greeting each other with a kiss on the cheek. With snow on my boots and my yellow power coat on, he looked down at me, brows raised, and asked in a teasing voice, "Are you ready?"

The more respectful this man was, the more I wanted him to *disrespect* me. I stood on tiptoe to kiss him on the cheek, my heart summersaulting as I did. He asked to take my coat. When he turned around to look at me, he paused, blinked, and—looking me up and down—said, "WOW. That's a really nice dress."

I hadn't realized that I hadn't worn a dress on any of our dates, and this mini fit and flare had gotten the strongest reaction out of him yet. Noted. I was *definitely* contemplating a sudden need for a few more dresses.

He gestured for me to follow him into the kitchen where his mother was feverishly whipping up a delicious dinner. I went over with my little bouquet in hand and asked if I could give her a hug. She was this teeny Italian-American woman who I towered over.

She paused to get a good look at me, her face lighting up. "Oh my gosh, you're beautiful!"

His dad sat at an island counter overlooking the kitchen. I moved to shake his hand.

His mom apologized because she'd tried out a new brand of pasta and she didn't know how it was going to go.

"Please don't apologize." I told her. "I love pasta. You can never go wrong with pasta."

She paused, leaning on the island counter to study me. "What's your nationality?"

"I'm Italian, Irish, and Puerto Rican."

She grinned, glanced over at Grant beside me. "Italian." She nodded in approval. Grant had been watching me get to know his parents as I bounced from topic to topic with only occasional additions from him. He leaned down at one point, mid-conversation, to tell me, "You can sit down, you know."

I leaned back towards him, whispering, "I'm honestly so nervous that I feel like I need to be moving around."

He nodded, amused. "Fair enough."

Nervous or not, it did, overall, feel so relaxed. I enjoyed, even when just meeting my friends' parents or family, seeing how they operated together. Not everybody gets along with their parents (which is fine), but I wanted to see what their dynamic was like. So far, it had been causal and relaxed. The food (a garlic shrimp number) filled the kitchen with a mouth-watering aroma. Wine was poured. Conversation flowed. In no time at all, I realized I was even having fun. Wild. I could tell that he also got along with his parents, as they talked to each other and told stories. The atmosphere was warm, enthusiastic, and inviting.

We eventually sat down for dinner. Grant started bragging about how I had made this TikTok channel that was taking off. On my end, I had not expected the flush of pride and pleasure at having him talk about me like that. It was unexpected and pretty damn cute.

We discussed hobbies and interests. They told me about his siblings, past family vacations, how I should get into football so that I could join them to watch the games. Go Bills! His dad, in turn, started bragging about his mom—how she was talented with knitting. She had made all these intricately designed blankets and such and—at one point—his dad got up from the table to show me some of her projects. He was so excited to tell me about some of his wife's accomplishments. I could see where Grant had gotten this particular trait.

The highlight of my evening, by far, was when Grant brought

up that I was a huge Elvis fan. His parents had seen the King in concert twice before. Half-jokingly, I took his mother's hand. "Can I hold your hand for a minute? Besides me actually visiting Grace-land, this is the closest to Elvis I've ever been."

She chuckled.

Once dinner ended, I was thwarted from sitting directly next to him by the armrests that broke up the large, brown sectional in their living room. Ordinarily, I wouldn't have been comfortable cozying right up to him in front of his parents. But it was alarming to me how, already, I felt hungry to be near him. Touch him. I had no chill. I hadn't seen him in a week and a half. This was the only downside of this date. I wanted more.

Grant turned on the TV, selecting the "Aloha from Hawaii" Elvis special to play in the background. "Seems fair after tonight's conversation," he told me.

I ate it up. I was delighted when his mom began pulling out photo albums and scrapbooks—pointing out baby Grant's child-hood misadventures. At one point, he got up to go to the bathroom, and I gestured for them both to lean in closer. "Alright. Give me the dirt. What kind of trouble did Grant get into as a kid?"

"Oh no," his mom said. "He was such a good kid. He never got into trouble. If anything, he was a little bit of a tattletale for his sisters. They were the ones getting into trouble, and he was the one letting us know about it."

We had dessert—a choice of warmed apple pie with a scoop of crisp vanilla ice cream or a chilled cheesecake. I chose a sliver of both, marveling, as we ate, at how normal this all felt. I never had to meet someone's parents before, and honestly, it was a lovely night. As the evening drew to a close, Grant retrieved my coat. His mom packed me up a little goodie bag of leftovers to take home.

Before I shrugged it on, I paused, pulling something out of my coat pocket. "I have something for you," I told him. He'd said on our last date that his hands were always dry from washing them so much at work. Growing up on a farm, I was familiar with the perils of dry skin in winter. My hands were always cracked and bleeding during the coldest months. But my mom was a Mary Kay lady, had been since I was a teenager, and she'd gotten us all hooked on this "Satin Hands" treatment that saved us every year. I gestured for him to follow me into the bathroom.

"This is going to save your skin, basically," I told him as he followed me inside. I paused by the sink, glancing up at him with my brows raised "Do you trust me?"

He quirked the corner of his mouth, his gaze warm. "Yes."

I reached for his hands, brushing my thumb over his knuckles as heat climbed up my neck. "Okay, so first we're going to rub this in —" I explained the three-step process. For each step, I took his hand, squeezed out the product, and—*WHO IS SHE?*—rubbed it into his skin as I avoided eye contact.

Post skin-care routine, I gave his parents warm goodbyes and quick hugs.

Grant walked me out to my car. The moment the door closed he let out a big exhale. "Oh wow, that went really well."

I beamed. "Did it? It felt like it was going well, but I wasn't sure."

We moved out of the line of sight of the doorway, within the circle of interior light from my car as I opened the door and started it up. It was frigid out. Our breaths curled on the crisp, night air as we huddled closer.

I reached up, encircling my arms around his neck for a big hug. "Honestly, this was really fun. When am I going to see you again, and can I get you to myself next time?"

"We'll figure it out later," he assured me, promising to text me details for our next date soon. I said nothing but was absolutely aware that Valentine's Day was only a week away. Although I didn't have any specific expectations for what that day should look like with a boyfriend, I craved every silly romantic gesture at the same time.

"Well, we should definitely have a little goodnight kiss," he said.

My panic must have been visible—he quickly followed up with, "Or not, don't worry about it." He took a step back, putting his hands behind him and grinned impishly. "I won't even touch you."

I could tell, despite his jovial tone, that he was serious about making me feel comfortable. He was poking fun at the situation—but not at me. And did that not light a *fucking fire* inside of me? I was nervous about kissing because I still didn't really know how to do it. But did I want all the kisses? Hell yes.

"No, no. Treat this normal," I said, more to myself than to him.

He took a step forward, sliding his arms around me, as I tucked my arms inside his coat. It was a short kiss, a press of lips between breaths of cool air. Sweet.

I didn't understand how I could still be afraid and yet crave him at the same time. I texted him once I got home and pressed him again for reassurance that his parents had liked me.

They did like you, and they were surprised when I told them afterwards how nervous you were. They couldn't tell, he texted back.

It is just so easy being around you, I told him, marveling again at this fact more than anything. *You're making it very hard for a girl not to catch feelings.*

Sounds like we're moving in the right direction then, he replied.

ARE you supposed to keep these thoughts to yourself when they feel like they are exploding inside of you? A part of me felt like a runaway train. I was doing my best to pump the brakes, but I hadn't expected to like someone so quickly. I wasn't expecting to be making room in my life for someone I barely knew.

I'd been expecting to go on several shitty dates and go online and tell everyone these funny stories to keep me brave and to keep me trying. Instead, every time I looked at him, he was getting more and more handsome. I was feeling more and more comfortable. And now I was figuring out what our next dates could be, when he would be meeting my family, when he would *kiss me again*. It was all alarming, and thrilling, and I felt so … alive.

I was doing my best to slow down. I didn't know if I was doing any of it right, or well. But I did know that I was having a good time and that my terror was abating a little more every day. I didn't care what we did next so long as we did it together.

Chapter 13

MOAN A LITTLE

For our fifth date, I invited him over to my house for a retro gaming night. I wasn't a gamer in any sense of the word, but he was, and I knew we could find common ground in some games I had played when I was kid. Our plan was to grab takeout, play a little *King's Quest* (an old PC game), snuggle, and watch a movie.

This time, some of my siblings were going to be around at the family homestead. I wanted him to start meeting them, and then for us to be left alone for the rest of the night. Ahead of time, he asked me to send names and short descriptions of anyone who might be around since my siblings stopped by the homestead unannounced all the time. That night, three of my sisters and a brother-in-law were around, so we decided to start tackling family introductions in drizzles.

The sun was still out when he arrived. I asked if he'd be game to go for a walk. The last time Grant had been over, my grumpy little dog, Digory, had been super standoffish. I, selfishly, really wanted my pup to like him. Bonding opportunities for the two of them were high on my priority list. And, wouldn't you know it, Digory snuggled right up to Grant for pets and brought him his favorite frisbee the moment we went outside. First signs of approval: check.

"From here, on a clear night, there's this huge expanse of sky," I told him as we paused on a hill overlooking the farm and surrounding valley. "You can see tons of stars."

"I can imagine that being really beautiful," he said. "I'd love to see your stars sometime."

I flushed with pleasure. We continued walking, Digory running ahead of us, the sun still shining. It all felt so normal. Effortless. Real. We tossed Digory's frisbee for a few minutes, then Grant and I meandered to the cars to pick up pizza. By the time we got back, my sisters were in the kitchen, a loud, warm, and welcoming gaggle.

They introduced themselves as I got him a drink. He offered everyone a slice of the pizza he'd ordered, which had just about every topping that you could possibly have. No one took him up on it. We were mostly a cheese or pepperoni kind of family. We all crowded around the island counter in the kitchen.

I knew Grant was a fairly chatty person, but it warmed my heart to see how quickly he dove into conversations with each of my sisters. My youngest sister loved horror movies, so they immediately hit it off there. My other sister was a gamer. We discovered they played a lot of the same games. My last sister asked him about his family, siblings, and what he did for work. Nothing felt forced. Between realizing that and diving into a glass of wine, I started to relax.

I'd also known, as the oldest of my siblings, that anyone I dated would likely be older than me (and hence considerably older than the rest of them). I'd worried that if I brought home someone older (Grant was four years older than me), that he'd feel old around them, or that he wouldn't get on with my family. But he was at ease around them. We were all laughing together. I could tell that they liked him, and, in turn, that he was comfortable around them.

One thing I had not expected to be a turn on: for your date to get along with your siblings. I was discovering new things as a late bloomer all the time. We finished dinner. Grant got up to use the bathroom. Once he was out of earshot, I turned and glared at each of my sisters in turn.

"Once that living room door closes," I warned, "nobody is

allowed to come in there. *Nobody.*" I know modern architecture capitalizes on open floor plans but, at the moment, I was grateful that the kitchen, dining room, and living room were all broken up into separate spaces with doors. Even though I'd made it perfectly clear to my parents that I would not be sneaking around and/or "waiting for marriage," my youngest sister, who was sixteen, still lived there.

So, at age 32, I was in the odd position of following the house rules we'd had in place as teenagers, which included no boyfriends sleeping over or being allowed upstairs in our bedrooms. Privacy in the living room was, to quote the great Ryan Gosling, "*Sublime.*"

We closed the living room door. I handed him my laptop and he set up *King's Quest.* As we sat beside each other on the couch, he told me that there were no character voices when the little dialogue boxes popped up. Like the little theater nerd that he was, Grant decided to perform all dialogue for the entirety of our game time. I giggled so hard I couldn't breathe. After an hour, we switched over to watching *Black Christmas.* The fact that it was one of Elvis' favorite horror movies was a bit of Elvis trivia I didn't know.

"You sit there." I pointed to the corner of the sectional. Remember, "best view of the TV." This time, your girl was not shy. I knew I wanted to cuddle and pressed right into his side.

He nodded, smirking. "Oh, we're cuddling, are we?"

I grinned, ignoring my flushing cheeks. "*Definitely* cuddling."

As I'd snuggled up to him, he asked, "You know, we could try practicing kissing now."

Although the suggestion thrilled me, I panicked. I did want to "practice" kissing—*very much.* It was hard to just "switch on" a new skill set like that. I didn't feel confident in what I was doing yet, and that made the attempts intimidating. Your girl was still nowhere near expert smooching level.

I groaned. "I'm sorry, honestly, can we build up to it? I'm not ready yet."

"That's okay," he replied. "We can cuddle and warm up."

Even though I was feeling *very* confident, I also didn't exactly know how to cuddle with a man. I don't know if all of you realize this, but those of you out there just raw-dogging your normie, relationship lives, it takes a lot of bravery to be physically close to someone when you don't have a lot of practice. As much as I craved it, and despite all of Grant's efforts to make me feel comfortable, it was still intimidating. I folded into the spot beneath his shoulder, my head on his chest. He slid an arm around me as my stomach flipped.

I glanced at his arm, then back up at him. "Your arm is going to fall asleep."

He chuckled. "No, it's not."

I couldn't stop worrying about it and proceeded to ask him three more times during the course of the movie.

After the fourth time, he replied, "You know, I was going to ask if this is the first time anyone's ever put their arm around your shoulders … but I just realized that the answer is probably yes, huh?"

Well, *obviously*, yes.

I've seen a few lightweight horror movies (in general, not really my thing—I scare super easily). My main gripe with horror movies, as a whole, is that they never seem to end well for the people you're rooting for. Spoiler alert: it doesn't end well for the folks in *Black Christmas*. We talked while watching, and I'd make predictions about who the killer was or who would die next. Grant tried to misdirect every guess to keep me on my toes.

By the time we got to the end, I turned and smacked his thigh (*WHO IS SHE?*), while reprimanding, "You let me watch this whole movie, *knowing* it wasn't going to end happily?"

The whole time you're watching you feel kind of unsettled, by design, I'm sure. My complaints only made him laugh.

Overall, cuddling did help. It was after 11 p.m. on a work night, which he pointed out.

"I really shouldn't keep you up past midnight, you have to be up early tomorrow morning." He was off the next day.

"Okay, *dad*." I snarked. "I asked you to be here, and I'm not in a rush. Okay?"

He nodded, hazel eyes amused, inviting. "Well, do you want to practice kissing *now*, then?"

Face flushed, I said yes.

Here's the thing about trying to jump into a kiss: how do *you* start? We were sitting side by side, and I was still tucked under his arm. I wasn't feeling stiff now, but I was nervous. *Very* nervous. I wanted to do this so badly, and was so irritated by my own hesitation, but I didn't know where to begin, what to move, where to touch, how to lean in and—

As if sensing the plunging line of my overthinking, he suggested, "I want you to be honest with me before we start. How has this been for you? How are you feeling right now? I know you've said that you're very 'skittish,' and we're still adjusting to touch and doing all this stuff. But, for example, when we were standing in the kitchen with your sisters, I thought about putting my hand on your back. Would you have been okay with that?"

My first thought was tinged with sadness. He was being so considerate, but it was another experience that my own fear had robbed me of. I didn't want to let it take anything else from me.

"Honestly?" I said, "I really appreciate you asking. Like, *very* much, but I kind of want you to take the lead. And I will be the first person to tell you if something is too fast, or too much, or too soon. But, in any other case," I blew out a breath, wincing, "Just, uh, do what your heart tells you? I'm trusting your instincts."

So far, he'd been proving himself to be reliable with those instincts. Green flag.

He nodded, turning towards me. He gently placed a kiss on my forehead and another on the tip of my nose. I giggled, barely breathing.

"See? This is alright." He turned to face me more fully. "Are you ready to do this?"

Eyes wide, I nodded. "Yes—I absolutely am."

We leaned towards each other, mouths parting, as we started to kiss. It was a longer kiss, longer than any others we'd had. My lips were soft beneath his, his kisses confident, but not dominating. His beard stubble, neatly trimmed, pressed lightly into my chin and cheeks. I willed myself to stay there, in that moment, and to not be intimidated by it. We broke apart for a second, catching our breaths.

"You're doing great," he told me, voice low and husky. "You're a very soft kisser."

I blinked. "Is that a good thing?"

He nodded. "A very good thing. You're doing great. When we go for this again, go slowly. You're like, kind of diving in for each kiss. Bracing for it. Move more slowly."

Feeling, with amazement, mostly mischievous and not at all self-conscious, I replied, "I can appreciate construction criticism. Let's go."

We kissed again, longer.

Slower.

I was starting to relax. His gentle assurances and occasional affirmations had me slowly unwinding. It made it all feel simple, his calm silencing the worrying voice in my head. He was sort of in "tutorial" mode, but also letting me feel the experience out.

It was perfect.

We shifted positions. He'd been leaning back against the couch. I was draped across his chest, our faces pressed together. The things I worried about the most?

1. *Am I doing this right?*
2. *Is this ok for you?*

The fact that he made it all feel light-hearted, giving me little tips along the way, made it fun. Easy. I was having a freaking *good* time. I asked every question that came to mind.

"What am I supposed to be doing with my hands?"

He considered this briefly. "Well, is there a part of me you want to touch?"

My eyes widened. "I—I—don't—"

Sensing my panic, he stopped me. "Why don't you try putting them on my shoulders, or in my hair?"

I paused, astonished by this prospect. I had no idea why I felt scandalized, because I loved when he put his hands in my hair. But in *his* hair? I'd never touched someone like this. Everything felt raw and electrified. I was sure I might combust at any moment. *I can do this. I know I can do this.*

Can I do this?

He offered an encouraging smile when I started to raise my hand and hesitated again. "Actually, I want you to do that," he assured me.

I studied his face, slowly letting my fingers extend, reaching and sliding them through his thick, dark hair. Utterly exhilarating.

Another moment passed.

He asked, "Is it ok if I kiss your neck?"

I nodded. Heat pooled as I tilted my chin. He pressed soft, gentle kisses along my jawline, and then lower, lower on my chest. My skin tingled, my whole body on fire.

"You can kiss my neck, too, if you want," he suggested. It was a little thing, those suggestions, but they gave me the confidence to explore, unwind, learn. I wanted to know it all. Between kisses we would pause, talk, snuggle. It was connection in a way that was different from holding hands or hugging. The consistent contact, physical closeness, and the heady intent behind every movement. The more I did it, the less it was about lips being mashed together and more about trying to get a taste of him, being in his space. It amazed me how intimate it all felt. Something I was sure people must be taking for granted, because, otherwise, how are you not all constantly kissing your partners all the time?

His little challenges continued. "I would nibble your earlobe," he told me. "But you're wearing a ton of earrings. You could try doing it to me."

I paused to process. "I … can do that?"

"Yeah. Give it a whirl."

I drifted closer, inhaling the cool, fresh scent of his cologne. Terrified, I let my front teeth graze the bottom of his earlobe before retreating. "I'm doing it bad."

"You're not doing it bad."

I wish this for every late bloomer: how he checked in on me, encouraged me, made me feel confident to stay in the moment, enjoy it all. We talked in between, mostly light conversation, with some trauma dumps and personal truths. One of the things I could not believe I was talking about, as I was draped across his chest, was *sex*. More importantly, my timeline on that. Did either of us have an expectation? He knew I needed to go slow, but I also needed him to know there was an inner sex goddess just waiting to be unleashed, but she hadn't made an appearance yet. "I want you to know you make me feel more comfortable every time we do this, but I'm not in a rush."

"That's ok. I don't like to rush sex either. It changes the dynamic. I want to take this slow as well."

Again, I had *literally* just said I wanted to take it slow. Those exact words came out of my mouth seconds ago. But as soon as he agreed? I thought, *right … slow.*

How slow, exactly?

Having a conversation to establish expectations seemed like a small thing, but I knew it wasn't. I couldn't believe I was feeling comfortable enough to talk about this. I also wasn't embarrassed by my own boundaries. How … just, how?

WHO IS SHE?

"Well, you said you want me to take the lead on things, right?"

"Oh yes."

"So do you want me to like, *really* kiss you?"

Confused, I frowned. "Uh, what have we been doing this whole time?"

I had wondered, after the experience of my first kiss, how "make outs" happen. We were having a good time—don't get me wrong—but these were slow, sweet kisses, slipped between vulnerable confessions, curled around laughter, swathed in comfort. It wasn't steamy.

"We can do this, but we're in agreement, right? We need to take sex slow? We're not doing anything else tonight?"

I could barely fathom kissing, let alone anything else. Feeling breathless and suddenly rather *hungry* for him, I nodded. "Yes." I didn't bat an eye and I stuck out my hand.

He smirked.

We shook on it.

He guided me as I reclined. He moved more on top of me and

started to kiss me. *Really* kiss me. There was intensity now. This—I realized—is what passion must feel like. His hands were in my hair, and I was *aflame*. We laughed into these kisses, the intensity and taste of them increasing my own desire. I wanted more, some, all, I couldn't decide. He kissed my neck and *oh my God—*

"You know," he said, "you haven't moaned at all."

My brows furrowed. "I—I mean, is that something people do? They moan?"

The shock on my face must have been profound, because he laughed. "Yes, if you're having a good time, and it feels right, you can moan a little."

But how did you *know* when it felt right?

He started kissing me harder, the pace and pressure increasing. He'd hovered above me up until this moment. "Is it ok if I touch you more?"

Absolutely yes, please. I nodded.

He sank lower until he was flush on top of me, the weight of him igniting something deep. "I might get hard," he warned. "I don't want to alarm you."

I grinned, feeling impish. "Sounds like a compliment."

"It's just biology."

That stung for reasons I chose not to examine too closely. "I'll still take the compliment."

Then we were kissing, kissing harder. Something unlocked inside of me that I didn't even know I had a key to. His hips thrust lightly against mine. I wriggled beneath him to a rhythm I didn't even know I knew, desperate for more of him, *all of him*, breathless between kisses as his hands grasped my side, trailing up my shoulders. I felt the hardness of him growing against my thighs and, as he traced fiery kisses down my neck again, on a sigh, I let out a little moan without even thinking about it.

He paused by my ear, chuckling lowly. "Ah—there it is."

I was amazed, as I paused to look up at him. For someone who overthinks everything, *how did I know how to do this?* It was a combination of my inner sex goddess clawing her away out but, also, his encouragement making me brave, setting my worries free. His respect for my comfort made this a 10/10 experience without making me feel like I was watching a "how-to" video.

"Alright, I want you to try getting on top of me now," he said.

"*What?*" At 5'9" and 270lbs, I had never been small. There wasn't a dainty bone in my body. I was okay with these things. I was *less* okay with the prospect of squishing him to death. "But I'll *crush* you."

"I promise you won't," he replied.

I cannot stress enough how it felt, as a plus-size woman, to be told that my size was irrelevant.

"Hey, stop worrying about it, okay? You're going to be fine."

Before I could protest, he slipped beside me, reclining against the back of the couch. I straddled this man's lap before I could think better of it. He gripped my thighs, his hands sliding up my sides as I leaned forward, my hands in his hair, kissing the hell out of him again, our hips rolling.

Who. Is. She?

I sat up and looked down at him. Some of my curls had escaped the low ponytail at the nape of my neck.

He looked up at me. "You know, you have this really sexy look on your face right now."

"*Do I?*" I blurted, wide-eyed.

"Yes, I've seen it a few times tonight," he said. "I love when you smile, but there's also this other face."

"*There is?* Are you being serious? That's something that's *happening?*"

"Oh yes, it's happening."

I swallowed, hard. "Well—I—the way you are looking at me right now, sir." I was sure I'd be a puddle in moments. Winding down from a kiss was also a new experience. The energy changes from something frenzied to something slower, comfortable, soothing. Breathless kisses transitioned to affectionate cuddling, and I slid off beside him, wrapping my arms around him.

His arms tightened around me as I rested my head on his chest. We laid there. He talked and talked and talked. He paused after a while, glancing down at me. "You're having a really good time right now, aren't you?"

"Yes." I sighed.

"You wanna know how I know?"

I nodded.

"You haven't said a word in like twenty minutes."

I was always worried about knowing what to say, or running out of things to say, that the fact that I could just sit in silence and be comfortable around him was a gift. It was 2:30 a.m. I was no longer worried. There wasn't a single thought in my head. I wasn't worried about doing it right or wrong, I was just doing it. And I did *not* want him to go. But I still lived with my parents, remember? Was I an adult? Absolutely. But I'd never brought anyone home before; I didn't know what rules applied to this situation. I also knew, even though they weren't home that night, that I could not ask him to stay without talking to them first. I wanted to be respectful of every-one's space.

"I should get going," he said. "You need to be up in four hours."

I did *not* want to move. "Just one more time?"

He didn't need much convincing to begin again. We kissed, this time laying side-by-side. Did you know there were so many kinds of kisses? It was a whole new world.

"Can you do me a favor?" he asked. "I would like to surprise you for Valentine's Day. But can you just keep that night open for me?"

Had I not always previously hated Valentine's Day? Yes. Had I tried, in years past, to take back my power and use it as a day to shower myself with treats and self-love? Also, yes. Was I looking forward to it for completely different reasons this year? Yes, yes, yes.

Grant collected his things. "I want you to know I want you to feel comfortable sharing whatever you want to share in your videos." It warmed my heart that he was so supportive of the content I was making.

Some people had told me, when I started making them, that I would eventually need to be more private, to save some things for myself. I agreed and intended to do just that. But I also knew, growing up, if I had heard even one late bloomer share their experiences, talk more openly about this, it would have changed everything for me.

Knowing that someone could be patient and kind, knowing that respect and consent could be so steamy, and I could learn what I did not know? It had given me a whole new perspective on mankind. I hadn't known, and I'd been so afraid. If I had known, it might have made me braver, sooner.

"My God," I whispered. "You're going to be the undoing of me."

"Ah—I hope not."

He kissed me goodbye and then he was gone. We were at the point now that, if we went our separate ways tomorrow, I would be so fucking sad. There was no avoiding that potential pain anymore. But these experiences? What was happening between us? I didn't just feel seen and heard, I felt safe. It was silencing all the worrying voices inside my head. It was making my world wider, brighter.

I wanted more.

Chapter 14

I'M GOING TO PASS AWAY FROM THE STRESS OF THIS

As single person, you survive the holiday and post-holiday blues, only to come up for air and get hit with a day that solely celebrates love. It packs a big punch for single folk for obvious reasons. I'd done "Galentine's" and treated myself to self-love days and my dad had given me a Valentine's Day card, every year, for as long as I could remember. But this was going to be my first time celebrating with someone I was dating. I had no idea what that was going to look like.

Grant and I had decided that we weren't going to eat out. As a former waitress, I knew eating out on a holiday was a 50/50 shot of being a total nightmare. If you've ever worked in food service, you know what I'm talking about. Holidays are always insanely busy: the kitchen always backed up, the waitstaff is exhausted, and the wait times are insane. Instead, I'd asked him to come over for dinner, and we'd have a repeat, of sorts, of our last "retro gaming" date night. That was the plan. Well, the plan changed.

The day before, he texted, *If it's ok, my parents would love to see the outside of your house. They don't have to come in or anything, but is it alright if they swing by while I'm there tomorrow?*

Stop it, of course they can come see the house, I replied. *We'll give them a mini tour. It'll be fine!*

Was it a little unconventional to have your first Valentine's Day involve your date's parents? Sure. But when had I ever been conventional? To make things even more interesting, after this conversation I found out that my own parents were also going to be home for Valentine's Day.

Not nerve wracking at all.

Despite living at home, I'd assumed my parents would be going out for the evening. And yes, they were, but they'd also be there, at the exact moment Grant and co. would be swinging by. Which meant that Grant was also going to meet my parents for the first time, and our parents would be meeting *each other*. It was, obviously, an increasingly "normal" situation. Which is what I tried to convince myself, anyway, as the day approached and I became more and more certain I would pass away from the stress of all of this. Brief introductions, a little tour, and then everyone would be on their way.

I worked remotely and told Grant that I'd be done around five. I had a meeting at 4:30 that I could not miss. "If you do get here a little early, just hang out downstairs," I told him. "And I'll be down there in a few minutes."

He texted me around 3:15 p.m., *I'm so sorry about this, but we're actually gonna be there at like 4:15.*

Okay … not ideal, but I could handle this. I threw on a new pink dress (purchased for this exact occasion) and ran downstairs to find my mom. She was sitting at her desk as I burst in and breathlessly begged, "Mom, help? Grant is on his way with his parents, and I have a meeting. Can you carry this for me for a few minutes?"

My mom, staring at me over the rim of her glasses, blinked slowly. "*Seriously*, Allora?"

I ignored her dry, disbelieving tone. "Don't pretend you don't live for this."

She shook her head, smiling. "Tell them it might be a big house, but we had a lot of kids," she replied sarcastically. "You don't come with a dowry."

I rolled my eyes.

Was this how I'd wanted our parents to all meet each other? Not really, but it would be fine. It had to be. By 4:10 I was pacing in my kitchen. A crescendo of panic built in my chest. 4:10, 4:11, 4:12— my parents both migrated to the kitchen, as well as a few unexpected siblings and my grandmother. I felt like I might implode by the time Grant pulled up.

Should I run out to say hello? Should I wait? Undecided, I burst out the door and picked up a jog towards their car. I was wearing a bright fuchsia dress, my curls wild, lips tinged pink to match. In short, I looked glorious. He got out and I stopped in front of him, shy all over again.

"Hi." My cheeks flushed.

"Hi," he replied before we gave each other a quick kiss. He'd texted me ahead of time to warn me that he had a sore throat and cough. *If you don't want me to come over tonight, that's fine.*

Even though your girl freaks over touching a gas pump handle, I apparently didn't care where Grant was concerned. *Please, for the love of God, still come over.*

Contagions be damned, I'd waited a long time for a proper Valentine's Day. A few germs weren't going to stop me. I gave both his parents a big hug and guided them towards the house. "Uh, don't be overwhelmed when you see everyone dressed up." I led them up the kitchen stairs. "They're about to leave for their own impending dates." They walked into a noisy herd of family members (around eight people). My parents shook Grant's hand. Introductions started flying around the room.

His mom shook her head. "Oh my gosh, there's so many names."

I leaned down, ready with one of my favorite big-family jokes. "Don't worry, there'll be a test later. We'll see how you do."

It was 4:30. I flew back up the stairs in time for my meeting. I signed on, turned on my camera, and started shaking my head as my team joined and started complimenting my pink attire.

"Y'all will not *believe* what's happening downstairs."

Did I explain the situation to them? Absolutely I did.

"Can't you just set your laptop up downstairs and leave it running so we can watch this unfold?" one co-worker joked.

"We're going to expect an update at our next meeting," my boss added, a wry smile on her face.

"Can we drill him?" Asked another. "Like, what he does for a living? What's he look like? We need to make sure he's all right for you."

I died laughing.

"Why didn't you just reschedule this meeting?" Another teased.

"For a *date*? When I'm supposed to lead this meeting? It's unprofessional!" Which, following an opening about my dating life, was ridiculous in retrospect. By the time we finished, everyone was like, "go get him tiger," and I ran back downstairs.

The parents had wine as my dad showed Grant's dad around the house and our moms stood together chatting. Most of my siblings had dispersed, so it was starting to thin out. Grant slipped outside, and by the time I poured myself a glass of wine, he returned with a whole bouquet of glittery red roses and a gigantic heart-shaped box of chocolates. Had I not always thought Valentine's Day was like the stupidest holiday? You bet. But was I now melting into a puddle? Absolutely. He handed me the roses and kissed me on the cheek, at which point our moms insisted on taking our picture like we were going to prom. Mercifully, that's when they started to depart. Did I want both our families to hit it off and be great friends? Of course! Did I want to get into my own Valentine's activities more in this moment? YES.

We were finally alone. Had that actually gone well? I hoped so, and I would debrief my parents later. I jumped straight into making us dinner: a cherry balsamic chicken with couscous, sliced almonds, and roasted carrots.

While my hands were busy, I worked up the courage to ask a question I'd been stuck on all day. "So … what do I call you … us … this?" I asked, cheeks heating, not brave enough to look him in the face.

"What do you mean?"

"Well, this feels like it's going somewhere, doesn't it? So, what does that make us, to each other? Are we dating? Are we …" I let the question trail off, feeling childish. Asking to give something a label, when we'd barely known each other for six weeks, felt silly. Impulsive, even. But it was a question that had been sparking through my brain all evening.

"Can I wait to answer that question after dinner?"

I glanced up at him, his eyes bright and warm, the promise of something in his expression. I smiled back. "Okay."

Dinner was lovely, and there was a part of me that enjoyed easing into this bit of feminine energy: wearing lipstick and a new pink dress with a Darth Vader apron strapped overtop, preparing a meal for someone as we talked about everything and nothing.

By the end he asked, "Can I do anything to help?"

"Want to take a stab at the dishes?"

He agreed without hesitation, and I offered him the apron, sliding it over his head before submerging his hands into the sudsy water. He didn't tie it.

"It's supposed to protect your clothes," I chided.

"It'll protect the front."

I didn't take no for an answer. I came up behind him and reached around his sides (*who is she?*) to tie it around his waist. My face was hot all over again as he washed and I dried, and then we bundled up for a nighttime stroll with Digory.

"I swear one of these days, the sky will be crystal clear here. I can't wait to show you in real life."

He shrugged beside me. "It's alright, it's something to look forward to."

It was such a small thing, that hopeful promise of something we would be doing together in the future. It warmed me all the way through as we walked, arm in arm, back to the house. I didn't let him go until we reached the door.

We were going to play the next section of *King's Quest* and watch another movie. It was my pick this time: *Willow*. It's a family favorite, where my name came from, and was something I'd fantasized about watching with a date for as long as I could remember. We also got cards for each other and decided to exchange them first.

I popped us some popcorn, grabbed the massive box of chocolates, and we headed for the living room.

"Do you want me to read it out loud?" he asked.

"Oh *God*, no." I replied. "Please don't."

One of the things I wrote? I thanked him for giving me many wonderful first experiences, and that I was looking forward to "seconds and thirds." Most importantly, I thanked him for making me believe in magic again.

"That was really beautiful," he said. "I didn't write as much in my card for you."

I told him not to worry as I slid my finger beneath the seal and pulled it out. It was a "popup" card with suggestions for what to do on Valentine's Day: "take down your Christmas decorations," "guess what's on the inside of chocolates," "loiter in the candy aisle and be reminded of how much you've bought." But at the end, he'd added: "BONUS ACTIVITY: do you want to try out being boyfriend and girlfriend? From, the Gentleman Caller."

I had always thought relationship labels sounded childish as you got older. But now? I felt like laughing or maybe crying as I was asked just that. In answer, I threw my arms around him in the biggest hug.

"Yes! *Obviously, yes.*"

We transitioned to playing games and snuggled up to watch our movie. I cuddled right into his side and loved how his arm felt wrapped around my shoulder. This date, so far, had been exceptionally sweet. As a touch-starved late bloomer, I will tell you right now that cuddling is criminally underrated and everything you hope it might be.

The comfort of intentional touch, of being in each other's space, was wildly disarming. It felt so ... comfortable—another marvel in and of itself—as I'd been initially terrified to be in the presence of this man. But here I was, laying my head on his chest, listening to him breathe. By the time we put on *Willow*, the first thought in my head?

This is a long movie. We don't usually kiss until the end of the movie.
Foolish girl.

In case you weren't sure, I know all the lines to *Willow*, okay? Grant hadn't watched it all the way through before, and I enjoyed every single one of his reactions as we experienced one of my favorite films. It was like weaving him into a part of my history. Eventually, *Willow* ended. My head was on his chest, his arms draped around my shoulders.

"I know you can like barely breathe right now, but just saying, I would still be very game to kiss you," I said matter-of-factly.

Did he do his best to talk me out of it? Yes.

Did I still not relent? Also, yes.

He leaned back against the couch. "This time," he said, "I'm not gonna tell you what to do."

I paused. Oh … I'm just supposed to *know* what to do? Just like that? The part of me worrying about this had *no freaking idea* what to do. Another part unfurled like a drowsy kitten in a patch of sunshine. That part of me led the way as I leaned forward, closed my eyes, and pressed a kiss to his lips. Every so often he'd pause and turn his head to the side. Did I register this as him *literally* coming up for air because he couldn't breathe through his nose? Nope. Instead, I only saw an invitation to the expanse of his jawline and exposed neck for neck kisses. I was making all kinds of new discoveries. For instance, there was also something *really* fun about making out in a dress. It might have had something to do with accessing my feminine energy, or something to do with Grant's hands drifting up my barred thigh as I straddled him.

"What else do you like? What do you want me to do?" he asked.

There weren't many thoughts in my head as I considered his question.

"Go with what feels right," he said before I could overthink it.

Obligingly, I'd give him a list. "Can you hover above me again? Put your hand on my thigh? Neck kiss?" There was something different about kissing him this time, something empowering. I wasn't being guided. I was asking for what I wanted, and I was taking every bit of it. I felt insatiable.

I started to feel guilty that I was having the time of my life, but he, you know, couldn't breathe. I suggested we cut our make out session a little short. But I had other things to consider, namely, tonight—unlike our previous dates, he was staying over.

My parents had agreed to let him spend the night so long as he stayed downstairs "until we get to know him better." We were all adults living in this house. I wanted to be respectful. I'd thought that concession more than fair until … the moment I needed to peel myself from his side. The house was quiet. We were cuddling again post-kiss around 2 a.m. Although I had taken time off from work that next morning, we did need to get *some* sleep. Saying goodnight and prying myself off of him felt like it might kill me. Once I'd made him up a bed on the couch, he'd walked me over to the doorway for a goodnight kiss. I dreamed all night that I was curled up next to him. Every time I woke up, I was curled up with a fucking pillow, pissed all over again.

By 8 a.m., I was wide awake, bright eyed and bushy-tailed. I made us farm fresh eggs on bagels with bacon and cheese. We snuggled on the couch afterwards. I could have stayed nestled in his arms for hours … and that's exactly what happened. We sat there talking or not talking. It was a quiet, calm moment in the face of all that had happened.

Even though I'd taken a half day, I was due to clock in soon. Originally, the plan was for him to depart after lunch when I went to work that afternoon. Regardless of any plan, I was already sad that he was leaving.

In the midst of cuddling he asked, "What would I do if I stayed longer today?"

I froze, looking up at him with an unexpected thrill of hope. I rattled off, "You could take a nap, watch TV, read, hang out after work—"

He chuckled at my enthusiasm.

"Have I convinced you to stay?" I asked.

"Is that what you were doing? Convincing me to stay?"

"Please … stay." I burrowed in more tightly against him, my heart swelling.

He stayed.

. . .

A WHILE later I headed into the kitchen to make us lunch. My brother-in-law was off work, and—seated at the island counter— he raised his brows as I walked in.

"Allora, haven't you been on your phone?"

I frowned. "What are you talking about?"

"You're in the *New York Post*."

I had been interviewed by a British newspaper, *The Sun*, the week prior, for a general awareness piece about late bloomers and my attempts to shed the stigma around the term. I'd forgotten about it, honestly—as ridiculous as that sounds. The story was published on Valentine's Day, and—apparently—global news outlets had picked it up.

My story.

My phone was blowing up with texts. Everyone was tagging me across social media. It wasn't just my TikTok community who knew my late bloomer secret now, it was everybody I'd ever known, people I'd never known, people across the entire *world*.

For a moment, one whole moment, it felt like the entire world could see me.

I hadn't realized that perception could be so terrifying.

Chapter 15

WHERE IS SHE?

Going viral for something as personal as, say, being a 32-year-old never-been-kissed virgin, felt a little like what Sauron's fiery eyeball beam probably felt like for Frodo. There was this moment where you are pinned in place by that perception. Suddenly, it felt like the whole world had opinions about how I'd lived my life and the choices I'd made to get me here. For someone who'd lived fairly invisibly until now, it was a wild place to be. The Eye of Sauron was scorching down on me, and I was just a little hobbit trying to duck behind a rock.

At first, it was kind of thrilling. I remember showing Grant my phone, marveling at this wild turn of events, and then not thinking anything more of it. But in the following 48 hours, my status as a late bloomer had officially and forever been catapulted out into the world. Every friend, acquaintance, and relative read that article, tagged me in that article, congratulated me for being authentic/honest/brave. My DMs were flooded with messages from "gentlemen" offering to date me, love me, pop my cherry for me. So generous.

To top it off, when I'd provided pictures to the reporter for the article, I'd sent one of me and Digory. Harmless, right? Guess whose address AND phone number were clearly printed on his dog tag in said photo? I didn't realize until my phone was flooded with texts from unknown numbers, letting me know "I should be more careful," that they were "standing outside my window," that they would find my house and "fuck this stupid bitch up."

I wanted to hide. I stayed off social media, completely overwhelmed. I had no idea how to fix this. It took at least half a day before I realized I could probably contact the reporter who'd interviewed me for help.

She was apologetic and helpful. Her team got the picture taken down worldwide—just not before it had been up for a full day, and not before it felt like anyone could come bursting through every gigantic window in my house at any moment. It was the most exposed I'd ever felt. I was completely crippled by it. Crushed, like I couldn't draw a full breath.

In the weeks that followed, radio stations, podcasts, magazines, and more newspapers reached out to me, asking if I'd do interviews. My TikTok account grew. I felt like I was on this runaway train: wildly unprepared for all of it, winging my every step. Many people told me I could pause, take a break, hide from the world a bit. But I felt this odd sensation of responsibility. I was in a season of bravery. I could be brave for a little longer while I had this unexpected momentum. More importantly, I couldn't believe how far my story of being a late bloomer, and fighting that stigma, had reached. If I had heard just one person talk about being a late bloomer as a younger person, it might have changed my attitude towards my own life. I never meant to do anything other than to make myself braver, but before I retreated to my hobbit hole, it seemed like this was a small way I could do a little bit of good. But my anxiety spiked at an all-time high.

Taking long showers, lathering myself in lotions, reading books, watching TV, going for long walks—all of the things I normally did to de-stress didn't help. For weeks, my chest felt compacted, like wire wrapped around my rib cage that was gradually tightening, tightening, *tightening*. The only thing that seemed to take the edge off was my brand-new boyfriend. The moment he'd walk through the door to my house and wrap his arms around me was the most soothing source of calm. I realized, in surprise, that I was nervous about a lot of things, but I was not nervous about him.

You'd think we'd concentrate on doing a lot of calming activities after a week like that, right? Some cuddling? Kissing? Movie watching? Merry making? We did all of those things, of course, but when I found out both of my parents were going to be in town one night (a rarity that winter), I asked if Grant would be game to have dinner with them. A totally non-stressful proposal. To my surprise, Grant was game, but he did ask if he should be nervous.

"No, be *yourself*. They'll see the person I see in you, and they'll know why I like you." I meant every word, but it didn't mean that had absolved *myself* from worry.

We met my parents at one of their favorite restaurants, The Yard of Ale. From the moment we walked in and Grant shook my dad's hand, I was abuzz. I sat with my parents, in that restaurant, because we all knew that this man liked me, that this man was *dating* me. We'd begun to merge our timelines. Maybe it was happening too fast, but I couldn't have cared less. I'd waited my whole life for a dinner like this one.

My mom and Grant debated the toxicity of social media (oddly ironic) and movies before my dad, with a twinkle in his eye, slowly turned to me, and then turned his full attention to Grant. "Listen," he began, "this isn't a job interview, but we are here to get to know you better."

If he was nervous, I couldn't tell. His answers were suave and concise. He was honest. He didn't try and sugarcoat anything as my parents asked about his background, his job, career aspirations, and dreams. In a line of questioning that surprised me, my mother asked, "Well, what drew you to Allora's profile?"

"A combination of her photos—she came across very confident and knowing what she liked. She was passionate about her interests, and it showed." He glanced over at me, still serious, as he met my gaze. "I knew she was going to be interesting."

I don't think I stopped smiling the whole evening.

It was weird to be sitting across from my parents talking about what we both wanted, why we liked each other, and all these other "whys." I'd been keeping my parents mostly in the loop with my dating life, but this was different. This was sitting down with intent to not only get to know Grant, but to also see us interacting together. My parents were having a ball, okay? They were teasing each other and teasing us. It felt normal, and natural, and other-worldly at the same time, like a scene from a book I never thought I'd get to read. Ever.

The conversation turned to me. In an astounding turn of events, my story had garnered the attention of the *Drew Barrymore Show*. People had been commenting on my videos from the beginning, saying that I sounded like a modern-day Josie Geller from *Never Been Kissed*. Not long after that article was published, a producer from the show reached out, and asked to interview me to see if I had enough personality for TV.

At this point, it felt like an impossibility. People like me didn't go on TV. Grant started switching gears, morphing into my hype man. He bragged about me, saying how he knew I could do stuff like this from the moment he met me. My parents jumped right aboard the hype train too—as I blushed—and they discussed what this could mean for me, for any books I'd ever write (my lifelong dream was to be published), and how I was getting this special message out into the world. They all believed in me. I was unprepared, again, by the pride oozing off Grant in particular. His enthusiasm was infectious.

When he got up to go to the bathroom, I pressed both parents for the initial impressions. This was, so far, the most time they'd spend with the both of us. My mom squeezed my hand across the candlelit table.

"He's really sweet, Allora. He genuinely seems to want to support you. That's not something a lot of men might feel comfort-able with—having their partner in the spotlight like this."

Dinner came to an end. Grant and I departed a little bit before my parents, who lingered to finish their wine. The moment the restaurant door closed behind us, I threw my arms around him in a crushing hug.

"Oh my *god*, that went so well. You did so good. It wasn't a test, but you were *so* good."

"Thanks. You didn't really tell me if I should say, you know, anything specific or not say anything specific."

"Of course, I didn't. I knew you would be great."

He had been great, which was another new experience for me. Having someone in your corner. Having him, specifically, in mine.

He felt like *my* person.

I'd never watched *Never Been Kissed* but, given the circumstances, it felt appropriate. We cuddled on the couch to watch it once we got back, the stress of the last few weeks fading the longer I sat, entwined, with him. Once it ended, we kissed—soft, gentle kisses. Per usual, I was insatiable. I wanted *more*.

I straddled his lap again. But I realized, at some point, that I was shaking. I didn't know if it was from the last few days catching up to me, but my legs and hands started shaking. He pulled away from me slightly, looking up into my face as his hands slid down the sides of my arms.

"Whoa—whoa, what's happening right now?" he asked.

Mortified, I slid straight off of him. I didn't want to cry, but tears burned in my eyes as my hands trembled.

He pulled me into his arms, so that I was lying with my head on his chest, my ear above his heart. "Is this because of what's going on? We don't need to force anything—"

"No, no. This isn't you, I—I'm just frustrated with myself because I *want* this. I want to enjoy being here with you. But this is all still so … new. I'm not used to having anyone to lean on." I closed my eyes and tucked my nose beneath his chin. It wasn't that I didn't have a wonderful support structure. My whole life I'd been blessed with family and close-knit friends. This was different.

"You know," he breathed into my hair. "I would do anything to help you make your dreams come true."

What does a girl even say to that? What's a girl, a longtime invisible, lonely girl, supposed to even *think*? I'd been pushing through every fear and comfort zone I'd ever known, being thrust into new and intimidating situations. I was on the precipice of massive life changes, but it somehow felt all out of my control. I tried to explain, but mostly I just closed my eyes and listened to the steady *thump-thump-thump* of his heartbeat as he talked about what he was feeling, what he hoped, what he wanted, anything—everything. I just listened, and I was calming down—my hands stilling.

Who is she? She was curled up on a man's chest, saying everything that has ever been in her heart, everything she'd worried about.

"I feel like you're scared."

"Yes." The admission clogged my throat. "But I'm not scared of *you*."

I felt like I was too much, like we were too new. I had been leaning on him hard, and I wasn't used to leaning on anyone. I felt guilty for requiring this much of him, guilty that we were not a simple story. I had made it big. Complicated.

"But that's what relationships are for," he replied. "You are not too much; *this* is not too much."

I felt like I could fall asleep right there. But *oh* I wanted kisses, I wanted *all* the kisses—which I told him, still feeling self-conscious over my teeny Menty B.

He looked at me, smirking. "Well, *who* is she? *Where* is she? I know *she's* in there."

I stared back, astounded, and speechless. I knew he watched my TikToks from time to time, but he'd never said that little catchphrase of mine before. It popped the tension. I tangled my fingers in his hair when I finally discovered where *she* had been hiding.

Grant came over the following weekend, too, after I had nailed a "personality" interview with the *Drew Barrymore Show* producer. I was going to be on TV. There are those of you who might have found this exciting. A girl, after all, does not get invited to be interviewed by the iconic *Drew Fucking Barrymore* every day. But this girl? This girl was willing and excited, but mostly scared shitless.

Over the course of a month, I dropped about ten pounds. I was barely sleeping and barely eating. I had no appetite. I couldn't seem to evict that bundle of anxiety that had taken up permanent residence beneath my sternum. Oddly, the only thing that did seem to do anything to settle me was quality time with Grant.

"We're just going to spend the weekends doing things to make you feel better," he assured me.

That sounded like music to my ears. I didn't care where we were, or what we did, so long as we were together. We planned a few cute dates: dinner and a night out shopping for new records to add to my Elvis collection on Friday (I bought two), an afternoon adventure with my nephews on Saturday to see a travelling dinosaur exhibit (Grant was endlessly endearing with them), and then the evening to ourselves. That particular weekend I let him know that my parents would not be home, and would he maybe want to sleep-over … in my room … with me?

Grant said yes.

I WAS GIDDY. That was the only word to describe the absolute and utter delight I felt in inviting a man, a *whole ass man*, to spend the night with me. It was, full disclosure, an invitation to spend a *nonsexual* night with me. Despite the fact that I was feeling braver all the time, we were still determined to take things slow.

It wasn't about sex, but it was about intimacy.

We headed upstairs after dinner and a bout of *Super Mario* (the only game I ever truly felt like playing). I changed into an oversized shirt that slid off one shoulder and tight, black sleep shorts. He wore a crewneck and slid off his jeans revealing boxers.

"So, here are the rules," I pointed to the mound of fur that was Digory sleeping on my side of the bed. "There's just one, really. Don't walk over to this side of the bed, or Digory will eat you." I was half-serious—Digory was a territorial little shit—but I also wanted to break the tension. There was a moment of awkwardness as we stood there, on opposite sides of the bed. Waiting. Neither of us looking at the other. "I know why I'm nervous," I continued, "but if I didn't know any better, I'd say you seem kind of seem nervous, too." I walked over to his side, sliding my arms around him from behind in a tight hug. "Is everything okay?"

He chewed his lip, still staring at the bed. "You're doing something you've never done for the first time, right?"

I nodded, pressing my chin into his shoulder.

"So, you're nervous. But I'm ... replacing memories. It's different."

He seemed sad, a contemplative look stealing across his face.

I didn't push it as I walked back over to my side of the bed and slipped beneath the covers waiting for him to join me.

As he slid into bed, we curled up on our sides facing each other.

I was amazed. "It's wild. I didn't even know your name two months ago. And now? It feels like I hit like fast forward on feeling safe with you." I snuggled up to him, my head on his chest, his fingers tracing long lines up and down my back as *Batman: The Animated Series* played in the background.

We disentangled as we started to fall asleep. He flipped to his side. I pressed my back up against his. I slept well for someone who'd never had a man in her bed before.

Any time I woke up, I reached for him.

I PLANNED a whole speech for the moment I knew I wanted to say "I love you." It was a chilly night in early March, and I'd been plotting it all day. Throughout our entire date it felt like it could burst out of me at any moment. In the end, as we'd kissed goodbye outside his house, it came out in a tumble.

"I had this whole thing prepared, what I was going to say," I blurted before I lost my nerve.

He paused, his hands thrust into his coat pockets, breath misting on night air.

"But I've made space in my heart for you, Grant. I—I love you." I practically ran back to the side of my car as I said it, pointing at him as I opened my car door. "And don't you dare say it back until you mean it."

He looked torn. "I'm not ready yet, Allora, but I will be. S*oon*."

I worried about everything but, oddly, I wasn't worried about this. If it was meant to happen, it would happen. My part was out in the air: a declaration. I'd made my intent and feelings known. I texted him the whole speech later anyway. In my opinion, one should never waste a good "I love you" speech.

I don't care if this is too soon.

I have made space in my heart for you. I care about what you think and feel. About who you are, what you've done, and what you will do. I want to understand the dreams you've left behind, the dreams you've yet to dream, and I made space in my heart for your dreams alongside my own. I want to know what lifts you up or tears you down. I want to always be in your corner.

I believe in you. I believe you. I trust you.

Life can change in an instant, and I don't believe in not saying something when you had the chance to. I don't care if this is for now, for a season, or forever. You are exactly who I needed you to be. That is love for me. I love you.

And you better not even almost fucking say it back until you mean it.

Chapter 16

THE NEVER BEEN KISSED OF IT ALL

The rest of March passed in an agony waiting for the *Drew Barrymore Show* to happen. Don't get me wrong, I was honored to have been asked. A part of me truly thought there was no way it would happen. I picked out dresses, told no one outside of my immediate family and friends until a week before, and leaned heavily on Grant for emotional support as my anxiety worsened. I was nervous about the whole thing, *meeting* Drew, *talking* to Drew, being on television.

"Would you come with me, if I asked?" I said to Grant one night, pacing back and forth in my office as I explained all the details. "I feel like I want you there."

He agreed. The producers loved the spin of him being in my corner so much they also invited him to be a part of the segment. They flew both of us to New York City, had a car waiting to pick us up when we landed, and paid for a hotel room a few blocks away from the studio. Super normal first trip together.

"Is there anything in particular you want to see?" I asked. It was Grant's first time in the city. We landed in early afternoon the day before, and there was no way I was going to hang out in the hotel all day. I needed to burn off all this anxious energy.

"No, be my tour guide," he replied.

I'd been to the city many times, mostly to see concerts or plays, but I'd done a fair amount of exploring, too. I made a short list of touristy places we could visit and we headed out to explore. Grant hadn't realized there was, in fact, going to be so much walking involved. He'd brought a fashionable Timberland type boot option (*not* ideal walking shoes for seven hours across Manhattan)—but he was game otherwise. We went to Rockefeller Plaza, Times Square, and the Nintendo store. We stopped to say a prayer at St. Patrick's Cathedral, grabbed a quick burger at Rockefeller Plaza, and ended the night at The Edge, on the top of one of the buildings offering a 360 view of the city.

By the time we got back to the hotel, I was exhausted, but not exhausted enough to get any sleep. I was up every hour of the night. By 6 a.m., I gave up trying to sleep, got dressed, texted a slumbering Grant to let him know where I went, and grabbed breakfast from the hotel lobby.

Before I left, I found out that two lovely people who followed me on TikTok had gotten tickets to Drew's show to come and support me. It was a gesture so unexpectedly kind that I immediately said yes when one asked if she could meet up to say hello. This was a one hundred percent new experience. That kind of stuff never happened to me. It was uplifting to meet a kindred spirit on a day when I felt like I might spontaneously combust at any moment. After a quick convo and hug, I grabbed my book and headed for Central Park.

It was beautiful and sunny—a rarity for New York in April. I scaled some of the big rocks, crossed bridges, listened to musicians, and wandered around until 10 a.m. to collect Grant. We didn't need to be at the studio until 2 p.m., which meant there were many anxious hours left to burn.

His feet were sore from the day before. I suggested he hang back at the hotel and get ready while I continued to explore Central Park. Even if Grant was normally cool as a cucumber, I knew he was nervous, too. I didn't know what I thought would go wrong, but my chest felt tight. My heart pounded as I wondered: *How am I supposed to survive this?* I circled Central Park for two more hours, AirPods in, blasting the Elvis movie soundtrack. For the last 45 minutes I listened to "I Have Confidence" from *The Sound of Music* on repeat.

I have dealt with anxiety, to a degree, for most of my adult life. But those hours leading up to the interview were unlike anything I'd known before, like my chest would collapse under the strain. Once I got "gussied up" (a Grant phrase), I sat in a chair with him across from me on the bed. My hair was beautifully curled, my fuchsia dress steamed for wrinkles, my lips pressed together in a flat line.

Grant watched me intently. "Can I do anything to help?"

"No, actually you can't." I snapped, aggravated. I smoothed my dress over my bouncing knees. "You could tell me I look beautiful, but that's not something you're comfortable doing, is it?"

This was something we'd argued about before: that Grant felt uncomfortable giving physical compliments.

I sighed and rubbed my forehead. Bringing this up now wouldn't help anything. "I'm sorry, I'm just nervous."

He didn't say anything, reaching for the remote to turn on the TV instead. I winced.

"Can you just turn the volume way down? I can't listen to this right now."

He hesitated, selected an ambiance video, and leaned back on the bed. "Okay, so, what do you do when you're nervous?"

"I walk," I said, my patience thin. "Clearly, I've done so much walking in the last 24 hours."

"Well, you can't walk right now, so what do you do?"

Frowning, I considered that question. "We can try breathing exercises."

One of my sisters had given me a few suggestions for grounding techniques before I left home. She told me to listen to music and try to pick out each of the instruments in turn. I began doing that— listening, eyes closed, breathing in, breathing out, breathing in … and then it was time to go.

CBS Studios was right around the corner. I'd been told to bring a few outfit options just in case. We wheeled my little suitcase down the street, looking fly as hell, heading off to be on TV like totally normal people.

After a brief, heart-pounding wait in the lobby of the CBS building, one of the producers collected us and paused when he said hello, studying me.

"Is that an Elvis necklace?" he asked. "Do you like Elvis?"

I'd been wearing a "TCB" necklace, and out of all the questions I could have been asked in that moment where I could barely breathe, asking me about Elvis was a life saver.

He asked if I'd ever been to Memphis, or what books I'd read, and we had a true Elvis fangirl moment, okay? We headed up to Drew's level and, once we reached the lobby, there were giant posters of Drew everywhere as people bustled about back and forth. We were led down a long hallway of dressing rooms until we stopped beside a door with mine and Grant's names posted beside it. The room was adorable, with floral wallpaper, a shabby chic couch, an illuminated sign that said something like "let your star shine bright."

Another producer walked in. He opened his arms wide as he stepped through the door, a big smile on his face. "Oh my *god* you look gorgeous. You're gonna do great. How are you feeling? Are you nervous?"

"I am excited, but about ten percent of that is undercut by pure terror," I admitted, laughing.

"Don't worry, babe. We got you. If it's okay, let's review some of the potential questions we have written for your segment before we hand you over to hair and makeup." He let me know that Drew was very spontaneous. Sometimes she asked the scripted questions and sometimes she did her own thing. "It's okay if you're nervous," he added. "Don't try to be cool or try to hide your nerves. If you're feeling excited or emotional, let it show. That comes across beautifully on camera. You have an amazing personality and a great sense of humor. Just be you and Drew will eat that up."

It was exactly the sort of pep talk I needed. I didn't have enough energy to put on any kind of performance. I just hoped I didn't sound like a giggling idiot on stage.

We were escorted down to hair and makeup. I had styled my curls in a loose some up/some down hairstyle, aiming for big, beautiful volume. When I sat in front of the hair stylist, she grabbed a little bottle of hair oil and assured me, "Oh, your hair is stunning. We're not doing *anything* to this."

My normal makeup, even when I'm getting dressed up, is minimal. My makeup artist took it all off and did it again—but *better*. I still had an "everyday" look, but with eyebrows so defined and powerful that I could have conquered galaxies with them.

"What are you on for?" she asked.

My cheeks flushed. "I'm, it literally seems so silly to say, but I'm talking about being a late bloomer, meeting my boyfriend, and going a little viral on TikTok."

I glanced down at her list of people she's touching up for the day. There were all these pictures of different celebrities. *What am I even doing here? I don't belong here.* I kept chatting, gushing my gratitude all the while. I cannot tell you how wonderful every person we encountered was. Every single employee I met asked me if I was okay, assured me not to be nervous, let me know Drew would take care of me, that Drew was so kind.

"Can I get you anything?"

"Would you like some water?"

"Do you need to know where the bathroom is?"

Once we finished, the producer let us know that Jennifer Garner was up (the guest before my segment) and he turned on a little TV in the corner of the room. I couldn't stand looking at Drew's beautiful face—it was only making me more nervous. I jokingly told him as much and he laughed before leaving me and Grant on our own, letting us know he'd come back to get us when it was time.

All mic'd up, we paced in circles around each other and the room. Grant wasn't as anxious as I was, and he kept cracking jokes to lighten the mood.

He stood before me, meeting my gaze. "I want to give you a hug, but we're wearing mics. Are we going ruin them?"

I sighed. "I don't care. *Please* give me a hug."

He squeezed me tight, mics and all. If I had known all of this was going to happen when I posted that first TikTok, would I have still done it? Maybe yes? Regardless, I was doing it—just doing it absolutely petrified. My heart hammered, my skin felt cold, my knees jumped in a constant bounce. All of it quieted when Grant hugged me.

Then it was time.

A producer led us up to the backside of the stage. There was a huge wall with wires everywhere and monitors showing the brilliantly lit room beyond. I could hear the audience clapping, cheering, the lilt of Drew's magical voice as she finished up the segment before ours. We stopped before a big set of yellow doors. The mic lady came up to check our equipment. The hair and makeup lady arrived for last minute touch ups, smiling as she assured me, "You look beautiful, don't worry about it."

I must have looked *very* worried about it.

Grant came up behind me and slipped his arm around my waist. He whispered in my ear, "Hey, are you doing okay?"

"I'm *so* nervous," I whispered back.

"Don't worry, you're gonna be great, you got this." He leaned in closer, his whisper raising goosebumps on my neck. "By the way, *I love you.*"

I love you.

I love you … *right now?*

It was the sweetest thing to say, but I was at my emotional limit. I turned to him, eyes wide and disbelieving as I spluttered, "You're gonna say this *now?*"

The doors opened.

I could hear Drew saying, "A 32-year-old woman posted on TikTok that she had never been kissed, and she wanted to go on eight dates by Easter. Did she do it? Let's bring out Allora Dannon." I could hear them playing clips from my first TikTok, talking about how I had never been kissed, never been asked out, never been on a date.

There was a huge studio audience—or at least, it seemed huge. 100 or so people filled in stacked rows on our left. Drew and her co-host, Ross, were on stage, illuminated under golden lights. They led

Grant to the front row of couches as I was ushered over to the stage while my video finished playing. My story was a part of a segment called "Drew's News," and she was seated behind a desk on one side, Ross on the other. I was meant to sit between them.

The camera crew moved their equipment. People shuffled around, working, glancing my way, waving, telling me, *"You've got this. Don't be nervous. You're gonna do great."*

I was surrounded by a sea of the nicest people all working together to produce something so in tune with each other, so effortlessly.

Another lady walked over, entwining her arm in mine, and patted my hand. "Don't worry," she said, "I got you. I'll tell you what to do."

I held on to her for dear life as she guided me onstage.

The audience applauded.

Drew called my name.

They wheeled a chair out for me.

Ross turned to me with the warmest smile, arms wide. "Thank you so much for being here. Can I hug you?"

I told him *absolutely* yes.

"You're going to sit right here between us." He gestured to the chair. "And that little mug that's right there? That's water for you."

My TikTok was still playing, so there was a brief moment where we were not being filmed and it was my chance to say hello. As I turned from Ross, Drew bounded over—the glorious, ethereal angel that she is—in one of her iconic power suits. Flowy jacket, flowy blouse, her long, glorious hair.

"Hi Allora! I'm Drew," she said brightly.

I responded breathlessly, "Hi Drew Barrymore, can I give you a hug?"

She gave the biggest smile. "I'd be *so* sad if you didn't."

She's a fairly small person, but I melted right into that hug.

She guided me to the seat. I sat knee to knee beside her. All these people were in front of me watching, clapping, cheering me on. Grant was right in the front row, but I couldn't bring myself to meet his gaze. All at once, I felt so shy of his smile and the pride radiating from him as he looked back at me.

The cameras started rolling.

Drew turned to me. "So, you're 32, you've never been kissed. You're beautiful, but tell me, how did this never happen for you?"

I was hoping to be eloquent once I was speaking, but, instead, I felt flushed, giggly, silly. I rolled right into a gushed response. "I know it must sound absolutely ridiculous when you hear that."

She grabbed my arm, squeezing it as her brows furrowed. "Oh no, it just made me want to know you more. Can you tell us about your background?"

I started talking about my siblings, being homeschooled, how my parents had this idea for us having this beautiful childhood on a farm-like oasis. But the longer dating didn't happen for me, the scarier it got, and instead, I concentrated on other things: school, travel, my family, my career.

She rested her chin on her fist. "Why do you think dating is scary?"

I gestured towards my chest. "Because you're literally scooping out this whole part of you, everything that you are, and you're like, 'Hey, here I am, love me as I am.' I don't want it if it's not that. I don't want to be with someone if they can't do that."

She nodded, smiling faintly. "That's beautiful."

She asked why I started posting my TikToks, which I quickly explained.

Ross asked, "What was your first date like?"

Smiling wide, I replied, "Well, it's absolutely ridiculous, but the first person who asked me out is Grant."

Ross's whole face lit up; he turned to the audience. "*Grant?* Grant is here with us today."

The audience erupted in applause and cheers as the camera panned to him sitting in the front row.

Drew turned to him. "What was your first date together like for you? Could you tell it was Allora's first date?"

The corner of Grant's mouth lifted as he replied with a calm confidence, "I was kind of picking up on that vibe throughout the first date, but she did tell me."

Drew went back and forth between the three of us, but Ross chimed in to ask me, "At the beginning of this year, you had never been kissed. Has that changed for you?"

I responded with a hair flip. It was cringey. It was glorious. I'd never felt more me in my entire life. "Oh, yes, it's my new favorite thing."

The audience exploded again—everyone cheering. It was hard not to feel a little silly. This was me—awkward, unfiltered, and unapologetically me. I was not sophisticated. I don't have a suave bone in my body. I was chipper and enthusiastic and raw.

Cheekily, Drew glanced at Grant. "Is Allora a good kisser?"

Grant replied, "After I kissed her for the first time, it made me like her more."

There was a small pause in our conversation. Drew looked at me again, her eyes starting to water. "It makes me so happy that people can be so gentle with each other. That makes me so happy to know that can still exist. It makes me so happy for *both* of you."

I couldn't remember all the questions she asked, and at least half were cut from the final interview that aired. I remember commiserating about the horrors of online dating, but most of it was a complete blur. Eventually, the interview came to a close.

Drew said, "We love hearing your story. Please stay in touch."

I laughed. "Whatever you need, Drew Barrymore! I'm there!"

She continued, "And we'd love to gift you with a night on the town."

I squealed. I think they edited it out, but it was so loud even she paused for a moment before adding, "If that's … okay?"

I hastily replied, "*Oh god yes*, that's okay."

"We're gifting you two tickets to go see *Moulin Rouge* on Broadway, and we're treating you to dinner out, so we hope you have a romantic night in the city. Thank you so much for sharing your story."

Unbeknownst to me, the producers had reached out to Grant and asked him for a shortlist of plays I might want to see during our time there. The realization that he'd been pressing me for an answer to that "hypothetical question" weeks before slammed into me with the full force of its sweetness. The audience applauded, the segment started to wrap up, and Drew offered for us to take some group pictures.

We stood in front of the news desk in a line: Ross, me, Grant and Drew. We took a group picture, but before she turned away, I asked, "Drew, I absolutely love this, but you're such a feminist icon. Do you mind if we just take a picture, just me and you together? Absolutely no shade to the gentlemen?"

She was game. I felt like my mouth was going to fall right off from how wide and hard I was smiling. Drew put her arm around me. I put my arm around her. I am a solid six inches taller than she is. She was stunning, her hair was soft, her skin felt soft, and she smelled *so* nice. I know I sound like such a creeper, but it was a stunning experience from start to finish for this country mouse.

I turned to her. "Your show is just such a force of positivity in the world. Thank you so much for everything that you're doing."

She took both my hands, squeezing them. "Thank you for saying that, and for your beautiful story. Thank you for being brave enough to share it with us and be here."

Then it was time for us to go. We walked out the door and everyone was clapping. I couldn't even look up. I held onto Grant's hand as we headed out the door. We were guided down the halls by the producers from earlier. They congratulated me, thanking me for being there, telling me I did such a great job. One of the producers waited for us once the doors closed behind us.

"You were great!" he said, grinning.

I hoped that was true. I had wanted to be eloquent, to let people know it's okay to be different, that everyone has their own story, that all of our narratives, no matter how varied and different they are, are valid. It's okay if we come to love at any time of our lives. Did any of that come out of my mouth? No. But I also didn't regret being my unfiltered, joyful self. It was like my happiness was a wave radiating from my chest.

Back in our dressing room, we were gifted our *Moulin Rouge* tickets and $200 in Visa gift cards for a dinner of our choice. By the time all was said and done, it was about 5 p.m. We grabbed my little roller suitcase, trucked back to the hotel, changed, and jumped into an Uber heading directly to the theater district for a night on the town courtesy of freaking Drew Barrymore.

The city was alive with bustle, noise, and sunshine. Many of the restaurants were packed with doors and windows wide open. We settled on a nice Italian place right around the corner from the theater, splitting a bottle of crisp Moscato and an order of savory crab cakes. Grant got a creamy alfredo. I sprung for penne alla vodka.

I sat there, across from him, clinked my wine glass with his and looked out into the city. *How the fuck did this just happen to me? How* was this our day? Like from start to finish, we were just on TV less than an hour ago. Then we were sitting there, with gift certificates from our lord and savior Drew Barrymore, just chilling. How was this *life* right now?

Who is she?

The *Moulin Rouge* set made me gasp. If you ever have the opportunity to go, *go*. Plush red velvet everywhere, the lights, the costumes, the *music*? It was pure spectacle and sexy and romantic. It took my breath away. At the end, confetti hearts rained in a flurry over the crowd while we clapped and encored. I plucked one out of the air to save, savoring the final moments of the most magical experience I'd ever had in my life.

We decided to brave a nighttime stroll back to the hotel. I looped my arm through Grant's as we stopped for a slice of New York pizza. As a fellow musical theater nerd, Grant wanted to go into a critique of the show, but I stopped his review midstride.

"Listen, I am on a happiness cloud. All you're allowed to talk about right now is what you *liked* about the show. We can save the critical analysis for tomorrow when we're back to reality."

After feasting, we got ready for bed, cuddled in the dark, and started kissing. I would love to tell you we had this zesty make-out session, but we were in such a haze. Because, what a *day*, what a *night*, what a *life*! Instead, we traded sweet, soft kisses, curled up together, listening to each other breathe. We talked for hours.

Dreamily, I asked, "Did that really just happen? You're going to make fun of me because I just couldn't wait for it to be over. But honestly? I'm a little sad that it is. Is that ridiculous?"

Grant laughed. "It's a little ridiculous after the month of nerves that you had, but I knew you'd be a little sad."

It had been an unexpected plot twist—and I had no idea what came next. But I was excited for it so long as we were together.

Chapter 17

"YOU'RE OVERSHARING"

The day before my Drew Barrymore interview aired, I jumped off the lawn mower. The air was crisp, the lawn an astounding shade of oversaturated green, the trees lining the yard still barren. I found my mom doing the most aggressive round of weeding I'd ever seen on the side of the house. Weeding wasn't usually a job my mom took on and certainly not at this pace. She stabbed her garden trowel into the earth and yanked out weeds. Stab. Yank. Repeat.

I sat down beneath one of our cherry trees, taking a long sip from my water bottle. "You don't have to do that, Mom. Give yourself a break."

She didn't pause or look up at me.

Stab, yank. Stab, yank.

"Are you okay?" I frowned.

"Did you look at your phone?" Sweat beaded her forehead.

Confused, I pulled it out of my pocket. There were two texts from her. The first contained a screenshot from my youngest sister. She had been texting a friend, making fun of me for making cringey videos about giving blowjobs, and she'd accidentally shared that screenshot with our parents.

The second was a long text from my mother, expressing her

profound shock at my choice to do so. She assured me I was setting an appalling example, that I was bringing shame to our family, that she didn't know what massive hole I must be trying to fill with my content, but this wasn't the way to do it.

My stomach dropped.

In the first case, I hadn't made a video about giving blowjobs— I'd made a video expressing surprise over how giving my first blowjob had made *me* feel. It was a subtle difference. Spoiler alert: I'd not given a particularly good blowjob. It had been my first time seeing a penis in person, and I'd been delighted by how Grant had responded. Those aspects had both thrilled and empowered me. Which is all to say, how *the hell* was I supposed to explain any of that to *my mother*?

Her weed pile grew and grew. We'd grown into friends as adults. I told her everything. Sure, we'd gotten mad at each other before, but it had never been like this. This *silence*. The initial shock morphed into a storm of my own. I felt hot. Fury boiled beneath my skin as I launched to my feet and stormed off.

"You have *nothing* to say?" She shouted after me.

"Seems like you already formed an opinion of me," I snapped back without turning around. I stomped through our kitchen door, thundering up the stairs. She was wrong, so incredibly wrong. My youngest sister was sitting on her bed on her phone when I stopped at her door, fuming. "I'm so glad my life is *such a fucking joke* to you."

Her head snapped up in surprise. I couldn't remember ever having been this angry, not at anyone. It felt like a tidal wave. What I chose to share was *my* business, *my* life, *my* story. I had every right to tell it. My sister was newly sixteen, and we were in the fledgling stages of connecting as actual sisters and less as me being another motherly figure in her life. A few days before, we sat on the hill over-looking the farm, watching the sun set over the valley, talking about where she wanted to go to college and what she wanted to study. She sent that text days later, never expecting me to see it. The sting of betrayal coursed hot through me.

"Allora what—what are you talking about?"

I didn't answer. I stomped down the hall towards my own room, slamming the door behind me and locking it when I heard her footsteps chasing after me.

"Allora … Allora? What's wrong? *What did I do?*"

"You *know* what you fucking did," I snarled back as she began to knock softly at first, and then more frantically.

"Allora, *please*." Her voice hitched.

I couldn't stomach the wholly new feeling of betrayal, ridicule, and misjudgment. I don't know how long she pleaded with me to let her in, how long before she started crying and retreated, how long before my mother followed me inside—furious as she called for me. We screamed at each other from opposite ends of the hallway. My sister sobbed a few doors down. I could count on one hand the number of times I'd ever spoken to anyone, let alone my mother, like that. I avoided confrontation at all costs, and it took a lot to make me angry. But there we were, hurling barbed words back and forth.

"Allora, are you, or are you not, talking about blowjobs on the internet?"

This made me pause, because the short answer was yes … sort of. As the months of my dating journey had progressed, my TikTok channel had become a video diary of sorts. I'd documented my first eight dates, yes, but I'd also documented my emotional reactions to all kinds of firsts: first time sleeping in the same bed together, first time shopping together, first time going to church, meeting my best friends, gardening together, but also more intimate experiences too, like the first time we made out, and, yes, the first time I'd given a blowjob.

My videos weren't play-by-play recaps or instructional in any way; they were about how I felt in those moments, what they meant to me, what fears or insecurities I had to overcome. They were stories I'd been sure were 100% mine to tell, and I thought I'd been classy about it. My content was designed to normalize and demystify, not to titillate or sensationalize.

It didn't matter.

"I—I didn't," I'd stuttered. "It wasn't explicitly said—"

"But it was *implied*, so that doesn't matter. What kind of content are you *making*, Allora? Do you understand the example you are setting? Your little sister saw that. Heard that. Is that what you want her to think about you? Is that what you want *us* to think about you?"

I didn't finish the conversation. I blew past her, down the stairs, and out the door, stopping only to grab my hiking boots and my dog, jumping in my car and peeling out of our gravel driveway, kicking up a cloud of dust.

I drove to the closest, hardest hike I could think of as my teenage sister started blowing up my phone with tearful, desperate apologies. She hadn't meant it. She was sorry.

I sent her a nasty reply that equated to "Fuck off" and "I thought we were friends."

I called Grant twice, but he didn't pick up. I called my best friend, walking higher, farther, faster, as the story came out between sobs and occasional curses.

I felt misjudged. This feeling I was unfamiliar with—another unexpected first—clamped around my throat. By the time Grant called me back, I was sobbing on the side of the trail. Digory curled up behind me. Grant, too, thought the whole thing had been blown out of proportion and that everything would be okay once we all calmed down. This wasn't me. This wasn't us. This wasn't how we operated or treated each other.

"This time was so different," I said. "We were all so angry. I can't go back there right now."

"Do you want to come over tonight?" he offered. "We can watch the interview together."

The interview. In the chaos I'd forgotten all about it premiering the following morning. "I don't care about the fucking interview. I wish I'd never done it."

He paused for a long, quiet moment. "Don't say that. You did something pretty incredible, Allora. Don't let anyone take that from you. We can still make it special."

That seemed doubtful, but I agreed, told him I'd swing by my house to pick up some clothes, and I'd be right over. I showered, packed a bag, didn't say a word to my sister or my mother, and stopped by the living room where my father was sitting on his own. He looked up at me as I came in, still calm, glancing at the back-pack in my hands.

"I'm going to Grant's for the night. I'll be back tomorrow."

My dad looked like he wanted to say something else but, after some hesitation, he nodded. "Be careful. I love you."

I left without another word and wouldn't speak to my mother or sister for another three weeks—the longest I'd ever gone without speaking to either of them.

When I showed up at Grant's door, he took one look at me and folded me into a tight hug. I didn't feel like doing anything besides crying. He held me until I fell asleep.

The next morning, I'd already taken off work to watch the inter-view, but I was dreading it. The whole thing felt awkward and tarnished, like everything I'd been doing had been stupid from the start.

Grant's mom took off from work, too, and brought us breakfast. Her commitment and enthusiasm to making that morning special for us was a kindness I'll never forget. Her presence underscored the fact that I was here with Grant and his family, not with my own.

I had hoped the interview would speak more to late bloomer awareness, but we'd focused on the sweetness of my budding rela-tionship instead—the *Never Been Kissed* of it all as Drew said. A part of me dreaded what that would all look like on screen. I had been myself. I'd had an amazing time. Drew had been warm and kind—so, really, it had been an incredible experience. Now that seemed … silly? Childish? Naïve?

Grant paced the whole time we watched. I curled up in a blanket on the couch, his mother held her phone up to record it. Overall, it was excruciating, but also exhilarating. I had done that—one of the scariest things I'd ever experienced. I'd made it through. My mom texted me to say she'd watched it with my sister and that I had done a great job. I knew that text was an olive branch, and I appreciated it. I regretted how angry I'd been with them both. But it didn't change that I was here, without them, and that such ugliness had passed between us. We would call a truce in the next few days, apologize to each other for letting things get ugly, but we were also at an impasse.

I believed, wholeheartedly, in what I was doing. I knew, as much as they were trying to, that my parents just did not. I left to go home shortly after.

Grant walked me to my car. "You've done something incredible, Allora. Something you should be proud of. Don't let anyone take that away from you."

I hugged him tight—this man I'd only known for four months. I promised I'd try, and I did, but it didn't shake the sadness attached to the memory. I did know, with growing certainty, that it was time to leave home.

I had been toying with the idea of moving out for a month. My parents had told my whole family the year before that they would, in the near future, be selling our family homestead. Although I'd known it would take them time to sell, I started feeling more and more restricted at home as my dating life had begun. Having a boyfriend sped up that process. As a teen, rules had been expected. As an adult, everything about them started to chafe, especially after this fight. I'd been preapproved for a mortgage the month before and had quietly started looking at houses. It felt like it was time to kick the process into high gear.

Grant and I were out for a walk one day along the trail that bordered the edge of our farm, when he'd asked, "Are you sure this is what you want? I mean, you told me when we met that taking over the farm had been your dream for forever."

"It was. But that was before, and this is now. My parents are going to sell the place, I can't afford to buy it, and it just feels like it's time."

I still wasn't speaking to my mom or my sister outside of the occasional curt text.

"You're going to make up with your family, Allora. You have to," Grant pressed. "Family is everything."

I agreed with him. My family was my world. Things had been said between us that couldn't be unsaid. My mother had called me an embarrassment. My sister had made fun of me behind my back.

Both of my parents hadn't come outright and asked me to stop making content—but the implication was there. That, more than anything, I could not abide.

"I feel like they're trying to silence me," I told him. "And I've been so careful not to tell other people's stories my whole life. For the first time, this is *my* story to tell. And I won't be silenced."

The thought alone was maddening. Here I was, shedding a shame I'd kept secret my entire life, all while connecting with others with shared experiences across the fucking globe, while also experiencing the highs and lows of being in a relationship. I'd felt like my life was exploding with opportunity, excitement, and yes, even love. Especially love. And that—through it all—I was changing people's lives, in some small way, by letting them know they weren't alone. Their experiences and sadness were valid. They were worthy. Most importantly, they were fully capable of changing their lives at any time.

Sharing my stories was not only cathartic and empowering, it also felt important—one of the most important things I'd ever done, strange as that may be. I could not—would not—give it up.

I started seeing around ten houses a weekend for the next few months. Sometimes Grant would come, sometimes he wouldn't. I appreciated his input into things, but I also felt that this was something I needed to do on my own. I wasn't trying to buy a house for us; I was buying it for *me*.

"Do we need to look at so many houses today?" he'd asked once. "I feel like four or five is my max."

I frowned. "I don't feel like you understand the urgency here."

I generally knew, in under ten minutes, if a house was meant for me.

He didn't seem to understand why I was pushing so hard for this. "They're not kicking you out."

I shook my head. "This fight was different. It's just time."

By May, I'd made at least 20 offers, and nothing had stuck. I'd spent Mother's Day with my family and things had felt more normal. Everyone was in high spirits. My parents and I had worked to put the fight behind us. I let it slip that I was looking at houses.

My mom was surprised, but also excited for me, like I'd made this decision without the fight ever happening.

I was more than happy to go along with it. I showed her some of the houses I'd been looking at. We marveled at how quickly everything was selling and talked about grown-up things like interest rates and the mortgage process. I'd managed to scrape together around $14K on my own for closing costs, emptying my savings and taking a withdrawal from my 401k.

It felt like things were going back to normal, and—more importantly—I felt like a grown-up. It was a feeling, I had realized, that I'd been chasing for years as a late bloomer. Even though the chances of actually getting a house felt slim, things started looking up.

Then another fight happened.

For most of my life, I'd been a textbook Virgo: eldest daughter, reliable, loyal, hardworking, trustworthy. I prided myself on those qualities, and I thrived on my parents' approval. Although my mother had told me countless times that I shouldn't be looking to find my worth in their approval, for most of my life, I had been happy to do so anyway. I can count the number of times I've ever fought with my parents on one hand. The second fight, coming less than two months after the first, was brutal.

I'd posted a video in which I'd talked about my emotions around finally being on the receiving end of crossing "third base" on my own and experiencing an orgasm with my partner. Having a literal orgasmic experience with someone else was new territory. It was like advancing to the next level of a game I hadn't realized I could play. Each intimate experience felt like it was building a stronger and stronger bridge between me and Grant.

I started this new video with a disclaimer that, although my content could be viewed by anyone, that didn't mean it was *meant* for everyone. In a conversation I'd had with my father after the first fight, when he'd asked if he should watch my TikToks, I'd answered, "Of course you can watch them, Dad. But they aren't meant for you."

In the wake of the last "zesty" video I posted, a few friends and family members had reached out to my parents to express their concerns around my content. "Does Allora really understand what she's putting out there?"

It infuriated me on multiple fronts. For one, I was 32 years old. Why were people still going to my parents if they were worried about me? And two, it felt like everyone was missing the point of what I was doing. I wasn't sensationalizing my experiences, but I was *sharing* them. I was sharing how I felt, the fears I had to overcome, the connection I was forging with Grant. It was something I had every right to do, and something that resonated with so many other late bloomers facing the same struggles and fears for the first time. In fact, the *only* person whose opinion I valued on the subject was Grant's. I ran all of my more sexually themed videos past him to make sure he was comfortable with what I was sharing.

I opened the video in question with the same content warning I'd given my father: "Of course you can watch my content, Dad, but it wasn't made for you." That statement blew my world up again.

This time there wasn't a fiery explosion of a fight. This time, my mother sent me a text, questioning how I could speak poorly of my own father on the internet. I was, honestly, completely bewildered.

"Have you seen the video, Mom? I don't say anything about Dad in it at all."

"But you told him not to watch it, is that right?"

Technically yes, I had, but only to steer supposedly well-meaning, but out of line, family members from calling up my parents to tattle—which, unsurprisingly, happened anyway. There was no screaming match, no blowout. But I could feel her disappointment and anger through increasingly agitated texts that recommended I move out sooner rather than later.

By the time I had a chance to sit down and talk to my dad, face to face, that weekend, I was angry and short-tempered all over again. I sat across our island countertop in the kitchen from him, tears burning in my eyes the moment we started talking. My father, calm as ever, wasn't angry. He was good at having difficult conversations with us, while also letting us know we were loved and letting us say our piece. If anything, he also looked sad.

"People said that you disrespected me on your channel," he said.

"I never have," I snapped. "Have they even *watched* my videos? I've never said a bad word about you or anyone." I hated how petulant I sounded. This conversation was long overdue because, as far as I was concerned, they were not treating me like an adult. I lived at home, yes, but I also paid rent. I contributed to the household, the property. I wasn't a teenager anymore and—worse—these reactions felt blown out of proportion.

He asked again, "Should I watch your videos?"

I sighed. 'Of course you can, Dad. I'm not ashamed of them, or what I'm doing. But, like I said, *I did not make them for you.* You and Mom met in high school. You've always had each other. I make those videos for people like me—who've been alone their entire lives. Who had no idea, for their whole lives, that there were other people out there like them. You have no idea—" My voice cracked, and I swiped at my tears. "You have *no idea* how alone I've been."

I knew he was listening, and that he was trying to understand. But I also knew we didn't necessarily agree either.

"That sounds like it was very hard for you," he said gently. "And it also sounds like you have your mind made up."

Lips pressed firmly together, I nodded sharply and willed myself not to cry.

"I know you can be very stubborn when your mind is made up," he continued, "but your decisions for your life are impacting mine and your mom's. It's just time for you to get your own place, honey. We'll do everything we can to help."

"I don't want your help," I seethed, heartbroken. Angry.

Dad nodded. "I know we disagree here, but we are just worried about you … oversharing."

It was hard to articulate the fact that I knew I was oversharing, but also how that transparency had freed me and connected me to so many other people. It felt like one of the most important things I'd ever done.

"I never said anything disrespectful about you, and I never will," I said, "but I also won't be silenced."

He nodded again, straightened, rounding the corner of the counter. I watched him move warily, my jaw working back and forth as I tried to hold back tears that, if fully loosed, felt like they'd never stop.

"We're family, Allora. If we don't have the right to tell you when we're worried, then who does? But we'll always be here for you. We'll always love you."

When he opened his arms for a hug, I melted right into them. I was still so hurt and angry. I hated that they didn't understand me or what I was doing. Even with us agreeing to disagree, the fact that I felt so far away from their pride and approval, something I'd always cherished, crushed me.

I clung to him for longer than I expected, and he hugged me tightly right back.

I HAD an offer accepted on a house a few weeks later. My parents gifted me the last $4K I still needed for closing costs. In the weeks leading up to the move, it felt like history had been rewritten. My mom and I were back on speaking terms, and my impending home ownership was talked about with pride and excitement like nothing had ever happened. My mom even made jokes occasionally about "the trash" I posted on TikTok.

One night, while my mom and I sipped wine submerged in their steaming hot tub, I sent her a collection of a few dozen screenshots of some of the thousands of comments and messages I'd received since I'd started posting videos. People thanked me for sharing, for helping them feel braver and less alone, for normalizing the conversation around the late bloomer experience.

"I didn't set out to do this," I told her, "But I'm helping people by just sharing my own story. More people than I've ever helped in my entire life. I know it's hard for you to understand, but that's why I believe so strongly in it. It's why I won't let it go."

She nodded slowly, contemplatively. I look the most like my

mother. We'd been partners and co-workers for six years running our clothing boutique together in my twenties. I'd gotten to know her in a way most of my other siblings hadn't.

Her dark eyes, so much like mine, studied me through the steam. "Do you feel like this is a sort of ministry for you?"

Relief overwhelmed me. Although this was something that had landed in my lap, it also called to me—I was helping people. "Yes."

"You have to admit, no one expected you to be talking about this stuff on the internet, right? Even you? The shock and awe of it has faded, and we are trying to understand." She paused. "We just don't want you to share something you'll regret one day. Something you can't take back."

I understood that she was trying to spare me from making a mistake, but I didn't see what I was doing that way. "I'm doing what I think is right. And I'm the only person who gets to decide that for me."

We hugged it out, topped off our drinks, and boiled away the last of those fights between us. We laughed. We gossiped. We were us again. I moved out a few weeks later. I couldn't seem to shake the feeling of being uprooted. My foundation had been rocked. I'd built my whole life around making decisions I knew my parents would be proud of.

I wasn't sure who I was outside of that.

And I didn't know how to figure it out.

"Make sure you take a video of your room before you move out," one of my sisters told me one afternoon.

"I've lived there a while," I joked back. "I know what it looks like."

She levelled a serious gaze at me, brows raised. "I'm serious, you're going to want to remember what it looked like. You'll regret it if you don't."

Her seriousness surprised me. I walked around my room a week before moving day, the first time I'd ever truly left home, videoing my space before I packed up my whole life. My emotions were a muddy tangle by the time moving day rolled in on August 1st.

I'd never been financially stable enough in my twenties to even dream of owning my own home, and I was ecstatic. Plus, I'd been chipping away at my childhood dream of inheriting the family homestead for some time. It wasn't so much that I'd outgrown said dream but realizing that I had no means to financially secure it for myself had made me reevaluate and make space to dream new dreams. In many ways, I was excited and ready to take this next, big adulting step.

Grant and my siblings showed up in force to help me move, exhaustion turning our giggles to hysteria as the day wore on. That night I slipped into bed beside him, tucking into his side, crying as he wrapped his arms around me. Once the moving truck was empty and my sisters had gone, I had not been prepared for the sharp crush of isolation nor how hauntingly empty this new house seemed.

I had also not been prepared to have someone around like this when I was sad. I was blessed by plenty of people who loved and supported me. But there was something different about having someone there at the end of a long, hard day, something about seeing your people rally to help you in a time in need, something about leaving home for the first time, something to feeling all that love, and all that isolation, as you embarked on a new adventure, something to realizing you are building yourself a brand-new dream.

Despite the tears, the exhaustion, and the grief, it all felt possible curled up with him, in the dark, as he helped hold me together.

Chapter 18

BUILD YOURSELF A NEW DREAM

I'm no stranger to building new dreams.

As kids, once we understood what speed limit signs were, my siblings were eagle-eyed when my parents drove us anywhere. I vividly remember one of my sisters, straining against her seatbelt, eyes glued to the speedometer, shouting, "DAD, you're going *too fast*. The sign says SPEED TIME 30!"

"Speed Time" became one of those random phrases permanently affixed in our family's lexicon. The phrase resurfaced, a few years ago, as I approached turning 30.

I hadn't dreaded turning 30. Was I thrilled? Not necessarily. Was I scared of getting older? Not so much. Was I finding myself measuring the last decade of my life and finding my efforts somewhat wanting? Yes, that would be more appropriate. I approached 30 like a mile marker for my life; this was as far as I had come, but not as far as I had to go. If anything, it made me stop and ask myself, "Is this where I want to be in all areas of my life?"

If my answer was no, what was I going to do about it? How could I build myself a new dream?

I happened to turn 30 in 2020 … which meant I had a whole lot of time on my hands to contemplate the current state of my life and what I wanted it to look like in the near future. I took the time to take my Speed Time "life check" into five main categories: health, family, work, passions, and dating.

#1. **Health**:

At the time, I was 370lbs. During my twenties, I'd lost and regained 100lbs. Approaching 30, I was the unhealthiest I'd ever been after getting burnt out on a super intense round of clean eating and exercise. I was tired of obsessing about my weight. I went on my first diet when I was fourteen and had never stopped. At 30, I knew I didn't want to continue obsessing about my weight, but unless I wanted to continue this trend—I needed to at least care a *little*. I started by changing one small habit at a time until they became a collection of better choices. For example, I'd need help this time to achieve my goals. My first two baby steps were:

A. Going for a physical for the first time in nine years so I could talk to my doctor about next steps.
B. I was addicted to fast food. In order to stick with healthy eating, I needed to like something healthier to replace it. I signed up for a meal prep kit (HelloFresh) as an experiment. The food I started making was so good that I didn't even crave takeout anymore.

There would never be a "cure-all" moment for my weight loss journey, but that decision to continue caring, little by little, lead to another 100lb weight loss. That initial step snowballed to all other areas of my life.

If the problem felt too big, what was a small way I could start?

#2. **Family**:

"I helped keep my siblings alive," I'd joke to strangers when sharing that I was the oldest of ten. As a pre-teen/teenager, I'd been proud to be my parents' right hand. I was considered dependable and reliable, someone who would do anything for her family. I adored my siblings. As an adult, I learned it was also something that made me unapproachable as a sister. That was a reality I struggled with.

When I was around fourteen, there was a strict "no dating until college" rule in our household. My parents wanted us to concentrate on ourselves (our studies, passions, interests) without the distraction of relationships. One night, one of my sisters asked me, "Hey Allora, what would you do if I told you Rain [her crush] kissed me?"

I didn't even look up. "I'd probably tell you to talk to Mom and Dad since we're not allowed to date. Why do you ask?" I replied without even a dollop of understanding that this was not a hypothetical question.

"No reason," she said.

Through my teens and early twenties, I happily assumed the role of lieutenant for my parents and happily assisted with whatever my siblings needed. I wanted them to always know *and feel* that I'd be there for them. It wasn't until my late twenties, as they started moving out, going to college, or getting married, that I began to understand that they didn't need me to take care of them anymore. What's more, although they'd always known I'd be there for them, many did not view me as a confidant or friend; I was just another authority figure. When I started to realize, around age 30, that they still didn't feel like they could come talk to me, my whole world shifted. I counted my siblings as some of my closest friends, and it hurt realizing they didn't view me the same way.

Until then, I hadn't realized how much of my identity had been built up around being a big sister. A new fear of being unwanted if I wasn't useful started to take hold. As did the knowledge that I wanted my family to feel comfortable sharing their lives with me, confiding in me, trusting me with what was in their hearts. But I didn't know how to change the pattern that had been built up through our shared history. Being vulnerable with my siblings and letting them vent about their lives without judgment began opening the door to creating the friendships I longed for. It was small, but it kicked off a series of events that changed my relationships with everyone for the better.

#3. **Work**:

For the last five years of my twenties, I'd run a fairly successful clothing boutique with my mother. We sold women's clothing through in-person pop-up shops and live broadcasts. It was an incredible experience: both being my own boss and having the unique opportunity to work with my mother. As year five approached, I was burnt out on the need for constant creativity, the stress of sales-based income, and the hit my self-esteem took as I got heavier and struggled modelling our clothing lines (a huge aspect of my job).

The financial stress had been one of my weight gain triggers in the first place, but—over time—it squeezed the joy out of something I loved doing. The thought of returning to the corporate world was daunting, but this current job no longer served me.

I needed a change.

It took a year to find a job and make the transition, but I did end up jumping back into the corporate world. The amazing team I worked with, the reduced stress levels, and the steady income let me know straight away that I'd made the right decision.

#4. **Passions**:

I'd dreamed of being a published author since the first time my childhood self became acquainted with the likes of Anne Shirley (*Anne of Green Gables*) and Jo March (*Little Women*). I hid in trees as a preteen to write stories, churning out fanfictions as my *Lord of the Rings* obsession blossomed with the Peter Jackson films. I went to college for creative writing, graduated with my MA, and published some short fiction in a few literary journals after graduate school.

Not long after grad school, the writing just ... stopped. I dabbled in a few projects here and there, kept a notebook of ideas and scribblings, but nothing matched the frenzied pace with which

I'd churned out fanfiction and poetry from age twelve to seventeen or the dedication to the craft I pursued in college. I couldn't seem to stick to any one project. Although I consumed literature at an enthusiastic pace, it was like my creative well had run dry.

In this singular way, COVID had a small silver lining. I dabbled here and there with different story ideas, but during the downtime and isolation of lockdown, I threw myself back into writing after a several years' hiatus. I completed the first draft of my first novel that summer. Once I started again, I couldn't stop.

Reconnecting with myself, my dreams, my passions was one of the brightest parts of my "speed time" check at 30. Reevaluating that passion made me braver. Two years later, I would travel to Scotland for a writing retreat with one of my favorite authors, and then to New York City to hone the pitch for my book. I made many amazing friends along the way and opened up my world in ways I couldn't have imagined.

#5. **Dating**:

Although I wouldn't take action on this particular facet of my "speed time" check for another few years, the question of "If I woke up in 30 years from now, and my life looked exactly the same, would I be okay with it?" *haunted* me.

I spent my twenties learning, growing, travelling, dreaming, exploring; becoming a better friend, daughter, sister, person, writer, building a life I loved and surrounding myself with people I wanted to share it with … but the answer to that question was no, I would not be okay waking up at 60 with the same life. With all these other "speed time" checks, I didn't know how to go about changing my life. I knew the first logical step was just to start, to take a thousand small steps in (what I hoped was) the right direction, and to pick myself up and try again until it felt like something was changing.

HOMEWORK:

If you woke up 30 years from now, and your life looked exactly the same, would you be okay with it?

- If yes, I'm so happy for you.
- If no, the exercise below is for you, babe.

Identify two to five areas of your life that you feel could use some attention. Is there a friend, hobby, or dream you wish you could reconnect with? Pursue? Achieve? A habit you want to break? **Write them down**. Below that, write the small step you can take this week to start a journey to change it.

BABY STEP #1:

_____

_____

_____

BABY STEP #2:

_____

_____

_____

BABY STEP #3:

_____

_____

_____

BABY STEP #4:

_____

_____

_____

. . .

BABY STEP #5:

_____

_____

_____

ONE OF THE things my parents instilled in me, throughout my life, is the power of dreaming. Creating new dreams, big or small, is an amazing way to flesh out your life. Stop living in the "prologue" waiting for life to happen. One of the ways my parents helped inspire us was through a "Dreaming Exercise" tradition my mom started several years ago, inspired by author Matthew Kelly.

On New Year's Eve, my mother would sit us down and pass out a piece of paper, an envelope, and a pen to each of us. She'd read aloud this series of twenty questions designed to help us develop new dreams—both big and small. Questions like: "What's a childhood interest/hobby you'd like to relearn or dive into again? "or "If you could live anywhere for a few months to reset your life, where would you go? "or "How would you like your loved ones to remember you?" We'd answer silently, share one or two that weren't too personal at the end, and then we'd seal our answers in an envelope and not look at them until the following year. It's an amazing way to dream up new dreams and to reflect on the year we'd collectively had.

THE PURSUIT of a singular dream can be exhausting. The "Dreaming Exercise" was meant to help broaden and enrich our lives. I've been doing it faithfully every New Year's Eve for the last eight years. Here's my bonus challenge to you: liven up your dreamscape. Write down your answers to the following "dreaming questions," seal up your answers, and check back in a year to see how far you've come. I'm rooting for you.

- #1. What's a childhood interest or hobby you'd like to relearn or dive into again?

- #2. Who would you love to reconnect with from your past?

- #3. If you could learn any language, which would you learn and why?

- #4. What are your top three dream travel destinations for the next three years?

- #5. If you could change one thing about your home or where you live, what would it be (i.e.: move to the forest and become a witch in the woods, build a new reading nook, tear down a wall, etc.)?

- #6. If you could live anywhere for a few months to reset your life, where would you go?

- #7. What self-care habit do you wish to grow in (i.e.: meditation, prayer, starting therapy, self-help books, going to church, etc.)?

- #8. What skill do you want to learn (i.e.: carpentry, changing a tire, web coding, etc.)?

- #9. Is there a hobby you're drawn to and would like to explore (i.e.: scrapbooking, rock climbing, journaling, photography, cross fit, etc.).

- #10. Although we do not "dream of labor," what would your dream job be?

- #11. What's one person/culture/time period you've always wanted to learn more about?

- #12. If you could improve or heal any of your current family/personal/professional relationships, which would it be?

- #13. If you could go to any concert tomorrow, what would it be?

- #14. What book or movie have you always wanted to see/read and never have?

- #15. What bad habit or addiction (big or small) would you like to conquer (i.e.: Doom scrolling? Substance abuse? Etc.?)

- #16. If you could overcome any fear, what would it be?

- #17. What's one limiting belief you want to leave behind?

- #18. How would you like your loved ones to remember you?

- #19. If you could write a thank you speech for your life, who would you acknowledge?

- #20. What dreams do you hope to accomplish in five years?

DOWNLOAD the full list of "Dreaming Exercise" questions at:

alloradannon.com/dreaming

Chapter 19

THIS IS, IN FACT, MY FIRST RODEO

For reasons outside of our control, Grant and I didn't see much of each other in July. We had a grand total of three dates where we went out and did something. There's nothing wrong with those kinds of dates, but going out meant no cuddling, little physical proximity, and, more annoyingly, little kissing. I'd gotten a little used to our weekend "date marathons." While not seeing each other regularly wasn't a crisis, it was a bummer. I missed him; I felt disconnected. Everything to do with relationships had intimidated me from the start. Months into dating, I still joked, whenever we saw each other, that I needed time to "thaw out."

We'd been having conversations about taking the "next step" with physical intimacy (a.k.a. sex). Despite my insecurities, Grant had been respectful and patient with going at my speed every step of the way. Even if I didn't feel like I knew what I was doing, I did know that this peach was 100% ripe for plucking. I wanted to be deflowered, my V-card cashed in, my cherry popped. I wanted to be a firsthand witness to "that's what she said."

Despite all those conversations, as he got into my car that night to kick off our weekend, he nonchalantly announced, "I think we're doing it tonight."

My eyes widened. A nervous laugh squeaked out of me. This was something I'd wanted—something that Grant knew I'd wanted —and something I'd built up a lot of courage for. But we'd just come out of a period where we hadn't seen much of each other, and, in some ways, it felt like starting from square one intimidation wise.

Because I'd started dating, people (myself included) expected all those insecurities to blow away like dandelion seeds. Poof—you're brave now! That's not how it works. I was equally nervous and thrilled by our impending sexcapade. Grant and I discussed a sort of game plan over dinner like a play-by-play. It might not sound romantic, but it demystified the experience. Knowing what to expect made me feel like I could do this. I was ready.

I knew that "first times" usually sucked. I was expecting that. What I did not expect, though, was how Grant went out of his way to make sure I was comfortable. I'd picked out a matching bra and underwear set—simple, black, lacey—that I felt comfortable in, and we skipped off to bed.

"I need you to be reassuring," I told him between kisses.

His fingers curled on my bra strap.

"You need to say sweet things."

"I can say sweet things." He trailed a line of fiery kisses down the side of my neck, along my collarbones, down my sternum.

"You need to thaw me out." I melted into his chest as we pressed together, feeling him hardening against me.

"I can thaw you out," he promised.

I knew it would probably hurt. I knew I would be scared. I knew he would never do anything if I wasn't feeling it. We were making out intently. Clothes were coming off. He hovered above me, asking twice if I was ready and twice I said no. I was scared, and I *wanted* him. I was shaking, I was ready—not ready—ready—not ready—and by the time I was brave enough (a solid 45 or so minutes later) the opportunity … passed.

I. Was. Mortified.

Crushed.

He slid off me as I started to tear up, my embarrassment

simmering into tremors as the whole of my body picked up on my failure. "I took too long," I whispered. "I'm so sorry.'

"Allora, *no*. It's not your fault at all, it's okay." He pulled me into a hug, running his hands up and down my arms as my tremors picked up steam. I cried. My whole body started to shake. I couldn't stop. I wanted so badly to have this experience with him, to make this night special. I had anticipated so many ways that this could be awkward. I'd never expected to be too scared to try at all though.

"We'll try again tomorrow, Allora, don't worry."

Knowing me, I knew I'd find a thousand ways to worry about something.

The next day we met up with one of his friends for a movie double feature: *Barbie* and *Oppenheimer (Barbie* for the win, obviously*)*. I took a shower once we got back, and normally we'd watch a movie, play a video game, or talk for a while before heading upstairs to cuddle.

But as soon as dinner was done, Grant looked up at me and asked, "I'd like to head upstairs. Is that okay?"

I thought he meant to cuddle, which I was game for. Once I got up to my bedroom, ambiance was playing on the TV. Whenever we kissed, we always put an ambiance video on in the background. My eyes widened—we would be diving right into sexy times.

I told him that I was going to try not to get lost in my head tonight. It was easy to spiral off into an anxiety cyclone, particularly where sex or physical intimacy was concerned. My brain constantly concocted new things to worry about: *was Grant only having sex for me (not because he wanted to)? Was I not beautiful enough? Was my body too soft? What if it hurt? What if he didn't fit? What if I hated it—what if, what if, what if.*

Fear had held me back from enough in life; I was determined not to let it take this. By the time we'd slipped into bed, I'd put up such a strong mental block that your girl was determined to get jiggy with it—for real this time. I *wanted* this to happen. I was deeply touched that Grant was ready to be there with me every step of the way.

Despite being a woman on a mission, at first, it all felt silly. We rolled around, laughed, made out, and teased each other. At one point, mid-kiss, the music from the fantasy-themed ambiance started to swell for an epic climax. We both stopped mid-kiss to laugh. There was something different about that night. It felt more natural and relaxed. As far as I was concerned, the most embarrassing thing had already happened the night before. I was ready to see where this new attempt would lead.

I felt feral by the time I felt him pressed up against me, hardening, whispering sweet things in my ear. I was not just thawing out; I was melting. His hands roamed up and down my back, kisses trailing my neck as his beard stubble tickled my heated skin. He'd accumulated a databank of how I love to be touched, and he was deploying every move in quick succession. I gasped when his fingers slipped into my hair, at the nape of my neck, my mouth soft, our kisses full of heavy intent.

His hand slid lower on my hip, toying with the band of my lace thong. "I need you to take these off," he said low, in my ear.

There was not a care in my head. I was naked, sliding beneath him, looking up into his face.

His eyes were warm, soft, sweet. He smiled.

I smiled back. "Hi." I cupped the sides of his face with my hands, meeting his gaze.

"Hi," he said back. "You're doing amazing. Are you ready?"

"I don't know," I whispered. "But let's go." I slid my hands down his shoulders, his back, guiding him into me. He was gentle, soft, slow.

I gasped, burying my face into his shoulder as those first thrusts sliced through me. The pain was sharp, fleeting, poignant.

"Do you want me to slow down?"

I nodded, biting my lip, knowing the pain would probably pass. I looked up into his face again, breathing deeply, trusting him completely. I breathed through it, my eyes widening as the sensation passed, replaced with something different—something that felt like building a bridge to him. I felt … *good*.

He moved slowly, making sure I was okay, and then a little harder, faster. He showered me with kisses when he pulled out, moving to pleasure me. There was something agonizingly glorious about how long it takes, how vulnerable you have to be, how connected someone giving you an orgasm can make you feel. I was loud when I climaxed against him, that kind of moan foreign in my own ears. My eyes watered.

It doesn't matter what anyone says; I will always put that kind of sex on a pedestal, because it was more than physical intimacy. It was the fact that I trusted someone, loved someone, enough to be here. This was a reality I thought I'd never have, with someone who knew the things that made me feel good and ready.

Afterwards, we curled up, entwined, still naked. I could not believe that there was not an ounce of self-consciousness in my entire body. After a lifetime of apologizing for existing in a plus-size body, to be naked with another person and unbothered by it, was so empowering. Sexy, even. When we eventually rolled over, our sides stiff, I fell asleep beside him. My back pressed up against his.

We cuddled when we woke up the next morning. We had a busy day planned. Sprawled against him, my cheek rested on his chest. I tilted my chin up to look up at him. "Can we … do that again tonight?"

He chuckled. "We can do that again tonight."

My answering grin was wide. After so much anticipation and fear, it finally occurred to me how *fun* and exhilarating sex could be.

And I wanted it all.

Chapter 20

11 THINGS I LEARNED ABOUT SEX

- **#1. Communicate with your partner if you're nervous.** The truth is everyone is nervous regardless of experience level. Whether or not this is your first time or first time with a new partner, you're learning how to do it with them and that's a new experience. As a late bloomer, this can feel like an impasse. You're already intimidated by a lack of experience and leaning on someone else feels gross. Just know that the right partner is out there, regardless of your gender or experience level, who will be happy to let you lean on them as you learn and grow in your own confidence.

- **#2. It is *okay* that you are not a sex expert.** Nobody is born an expert at anything. Physical intimacy, like everything else, takes practice. The practice can be mortifying. It can also be *really* fun. Be open to it. Be kind to yourself.

- **#3. Vulnerability is key.** If you are brand new to having sex, allowing someone else to give you the experience of pleasure can be intimidating. If you are someone who has explored what makes you feel good on your own, you already have an idea of what that entails, what gets you in the mood, what feels good, but that means you've also taught your brain how to do that all on your own. There is vulnerability in allowing someone else to do that for you, and it can take time to learn. It is okay. Be patient with yourself.

- **#4. Explore what you like.** On the flip side of this, if you have not taken the time to explore yourself with a vibrator or freestyling on your own, do that. It does make exploring sex with another person a little easier because you have a baseline of what you like. I'm talking specifically now to my ladies here: when in doubt, try a vibey new toy or a detachable shower head.

- **#5. LADIES: TAKE ALL THE TIME YOU NEED TO FINISH.** We can get in our heads—again speaking to my gals here—about taking too long to orgasm. The second you have that thought, it makes it even harder to get to the finish line. Remember though: it's not a race. You are allowed to feel selfish about enjoying your own pleasure. Tell your brain to shut up and luxuriate in these sensations. You deserve it!

- **#6. Things will go wrong and *that's okay*.** You are learning someone else's body and how you fit within that context for the first time. You're figuring out what bits go where, what feels good, what doesn't. Bodies aren't always elegant and neither is physical intimacy. You *will* be awkward. You *will* worry. Try and laugh it off. You are there to have a good time. Remind yourself of that. Life is not synchronized, and not everything always lines up the first time. It's okay. You will figure out what works for you along the way.

- **#7. Wear something that you feel confident in.**
  Something that makes you confident trumps wearing
  something that you *think* you need to wear to look sexy.
  For example, my high-waisted thongs (which hide my
  apron belly) or black booty shorts which make me feel
  1000% more powerful than lingerie sets. I feel more sexy
  in a flannel shirt than in a silk nightie. This can change
  and evolve with you, but listen to yourself. What do you
  feel amazing in?

- **#8. Sex can feel like a connection.** Physical
  intimacy, when mixed with emotional intimacy, can feel
  like building a bridge to someone in a way that nothing
  else can. I didn't know it could feel like that. I *love* that it
  can feel like that.

- **#9. Talking about sex shouldn't be taboo.** I have
  been able to talk to friends, sisters, even my mom about
  things that I thought I was struggling with alone, only to
  find out that not only they've had a similar experience,
  but they also might have solutions to said problem.
  Knowing I'm not alone is helpful. If you do not feel like
  you have someone in your life that you can ask those
  questions, I implore you to find a good support group.

- **#10. Open yourself up to the possibility that you
  are deserving of every pleasure *regardless* of
  any of your perceived physical or emotional
  flaws.** You are a glorious, stunning creature deserving
  of every pleasure this life has to offer, including this one.
  Yes, you can be scared. Yes, it's a vulnerable moment,
  but allow yourself to open yourself up to the possibility
  that you deserve and could enjoy it.

- **#11. Soft lighting/ambiance music helps.** Think
  about how hot you can look when you're in a dressing

room trying things on. It's because of the lighting, right? Same thing applies for sex. I love having some sort of ambiance on in the background for two reasons: one, the sound bodies make can be hot, but sometimes it can also take you out of the moment. For example, if I concentrate on the sound I make when kissing, I laugh. That is not optimal for foreplay. Having the music on is kind of like a soft overlay. It's helpful. Number two, you're already feeling exposed, right? Having that soft lighting is just gentler on you, okay? It can be soothing and make you feel a little less self-conscious.

Chapter 21

SEX, FUPAS, AND OTHER SOFT, ANXIOUS THINGS

"I don't want to talk about *not* orgasming right now," I said a few weeks after the first time I'd ever had sex. It was early September, shortly after my 33rd birthday. Grant and I had taken Digory for a walk.

He sighed. "We have to about it sometime, Allora."

The "it" in question, of course, was an issue he'd been trying to bring up for a few weeks—pretty much from the moment I traded in my "v-card."

"I don't want this in my head. Sex is intimidating enough without me worrying about whether or not I'll be able to orgasm."

"It happens sometimes, and I just want you to be ready if it does. Trust me, I have more relationship experience than you."

I didn't want to give myself something to worry about, but Grant preferred the control of tackling fears head on. His reminder that I was less experienced, something I was still insecure about, only further grated. I wanted nothing to do with his warnings. Having sex, and specifically having sex with someone I loved, was the most validating, powerful, and pleasurable experience I'd ever had. All of it was mind-blowingly addicting, while simultaneously terrifying.

I felt a little braver and a little more confident every time. That was in part because of me overcoming my fears and insecurities, but also in part because of him helping me feel comfortable. Going my speed. Even though I felt braver, it was also the most vulnerable I'd ever been. The mind games my brain played were vicious throughout the whole process. *Am I doing this right? Did I look stupid? Was I taking too long? Does he find me attractive? Is he doing this out of obligation? I'm scared.*

Although the thrill of exploring sexual intimacy carried me through our first few times together, it was becoming difficult for me to get out of my head. Orgasming, even with an attentive and patient partner, was taking longer and longer. One night it happened: the noise in my head won, numbing me completely to a sensation I thought I'd been building to. I tried to relax, to stay out of my head, but instead of release it all just built to ... panic.

Gasping, I told him to stop. He held me when my tremors took over, interrupting our night. When it happened again another night, and then again, I launched from the bed completely naked, drenched in sweat, and fighting against the rising tide of a full-blown panic attack. I couldn't catch my breath.

"I told you." Grant tried to calm me down. "It'll be ok. You're ok. This is normal."

I crawled back into bed, pressed my head to his chest, trying to breathe. It didn't matter what he told me or what he said now. All my brain could focus on was: *You're broken. You did this. You ruined this.*

I had no idea how to fix it.

Writing about it now, it's hard to remember the shame that intermingled in those first few months of sexual exploration. After a lifetime of being alone, I'd had to fight through many fears and insecurities as I adapted to being in a relationship. But building up to sex, forming the trust to explore something so intimate with someone else, that had felt like a true victory. I knew, logically, that having an orgasm was not evidence that my relationship was good or bad, or that I was good or bad at it. But after wanting to experience sex with someone I loved for so long, this seemed like some cruel joke. To overcome so much, only to ruin it all now.

"It doesn't mean it was bad or less special," Grant told me the next day. "I tried to warn you."

That only made it worse. He was saying he'd been trying to spare me from this worry, but I'd never worried about this at all until he put the thought there. It felt like buying your favorite ice cream on a blistering hot day, only for someone to smack it straight out of your hand after you'd had a single, glorious taste. I wanted more, but all the confidence I'd built up was gone.

I vented, sobbed, and debriefed my bestie while walking the border of my family's farm, looking out at swaying, golden hayfields bathed in late summer sun.

"Let me ask you something," she said. "Are you worried you won't orgasm from the moment you start getting frisky?"

I hadn't at first, but that answer was now a yes.

"Well, I'm going to stop you right there. If you tell yourself you can't or won't orgasm right out the gate, you won't. Your brain gets too loud worrying about it that you make it come true by default."

"But I've never, *and I mean never*, had trouble before on my own," I protested. "I come in minutes on my own even before Grant."

"Baby girl, of course you've never had trouble on your own. You've been figuring out self-pleasure for yourself your whole adult life. Right now, you're rewiring your brain to allow yourself to experience it with a partner. That's not easy. You're doing a great job. There are plenty of guys out there who wouldn't even care if you came or not. It's to Grant's credit that he cares enough about you to make your pleasure a priority."

Super chill girl-talk, right? Admittedly, both points were something I'd never considered. Regarding the latter, I was being intimate with someone—of course my needs would rank alongside his, right? *That* was uncommon? As for the former, the noise in my brain was always so loud with worry, especially during sex. That analogy made perfect sense. All I had to figure out was what to do about it.

"Can you sit with me?" I asked, sitting cross-legged before him as he climbed into bed. He groaned playfully and sat up to look across at me. I'd developed a foolproof plan for tricking my brain for tonight's spicy agenda. Foolproof because I was determined not to entertain the possibilities of other outcomes.

I thanked him for trying to make me feel better, safer, and for being a partner who prioritized how I felt. "And tonight," I said, "I have a plan—and I won't freak out regardless of the outcome."

His brows furrowed.

"These are the rules: You are here, with me, because you want to be. You are here because you are attracted to me and you want to have sex with me."

He half-smiled.

"Can you say that?" I asked, my expression serious.

He repeated after me, "I want to be here with you. I am attracted to you, and I want to have sex with you."

"I can take however long as I want, but it's okay if I don't finish. And you'll tell me sweet things to encourage me if it seems like I'm forgetting."

We kissed after my rules had been repeated and cemented, a promise that soothed my anxiety. He whispered sweet things to me when I begged, panting, desperate to stay present and quiet my brain. When I eventually climaxed, I pressed up against him, his mouth claiming mine in hungry kisses that I returned eagerly, joyfully—like fighting to reclaim a piece of myself I'd lost.

Just like that, having sex with Grant became my favorite thing in the whole world.

I began arriving at our sexcapades with a little wish list of fantasies I'd daydreamed of for longer than I'd care to admit. I bought my first black, silk robe, just so he could untie it and slide it off my shoulders.

"Kiss me against a wall?" I asked one night, my eyes widening as he hovered above me. My stomach flipped as he braced one arm against the door frame, his body pressed against mine.

"Can you kiss the back of my shoulder?" I asked another night. "Like, slide my bra strap out of the way?"

He looked down at me, a smirk hitching the corner of his mouth. Without another word, he spun me away from him, pulling my back against his chest. He traced his fingers down my sides, raising goosebumps down my arms as he tilted my head to the side and planted kisses down my neck, my stomach churning with excitement.

He chuckled, low, between kisses as I gasped, my eyes fluttering closed. "So … *predictable,*" he growled into my ear, my skin heating.

Sex became empowering, validating, *fun*—the strongest and most intense physical and emotional connection I'd ever had. Ever. "Can I do anything to make you … happy?" I asked one night, the question hesitant. I wanted to make it sound sexy, but I wasn't sure how. I hoped, at least, for some form of earnestness.

Grant shook his head. "Sex isn't as exciting for me as it is for you. I wish it was, but I've done this all before. Honestly, I enjoy making you happy more."

That landed heavily. I wanted my enthusiasm to carry us both. I wished it could. I wanted him to feel the same excitement I felt whenever sex was added to our weekend plans. The thought that it could never be exciting for him again though, even with me, always made me a little sad.

We knelt on my bed, facing each other. He towered above me, his eyes dark. For once, I felt small. His hand explored my back, sliding down beneath my shirt to grip my ass. My hands traced his shoulders, his chest, sinking into his hair as we kissed, his mouth, soft against mine, insistent, urgent. There was something hungry in our kisses, something that consumes. We were flush against each other—tender, but greedy.

"I'm going to take your shirt off." He reached for the hem at my hips.

My breath hitched when his fingers brushed the waistband of my pants. Goosebumps ignited down my skin as I stretched my arms up and he tugged my shirt over my head. He kissed me again before I could sling it off my wrists. I laughed into my answering kiss as I leaned into him. I reached for his own shirt. My heart pounded as I pulled it over his head in as fluid a movement as I could manage. He pulled the blankets down. I tugged off my pants before slipping in beneath him.

He gripped my thigh as I gasped, placing kisses along my leg and up my side. I moaned.

We tried a new position that didn't quite work. Instead of mortification, we laughed. Entwining. Kissing. Finding our way together and building a rhythm, I found myself constantly craving. I wanted more of him, of us. Sometimes I worried it would never be enough. I didn't know I could look into his eyes when he was inside me, that I could whisper "I love you" and mean it with every fiber of my being.

I didn't know it could be like this.

I bought lingerie sets for the first time: silken, lacey, frilly things that made me feel young, feminine, sexy. I rolled them out in bits and pieces, savoring any hint of reaction from him. One night, fairly tipsy, I unveiled a pale blue number with an intricate design of pastel butterflies and flowers lining the brassiere cups.

"Do you see the flowers? The butterflies?" I giggled, tracing my fingers across my chest and marveling at my own beauty—a new feeling in and of itself. My size didn't matter. My insecurities or inexperience didn't matter. All that mattered was that I felt pretty, like a confection, and I was excited to share that with him.

He snorted. "I promise you," he replied dryly, "no one is going to notice the butterflies and flowers."

I blinked up at him, a smile spreading across my face. Despite my own self-professed vanity, Grant rarely complimented my physical appearance. It was even more rare during sex, when it would have been appreciated the most. This tongue-in-cheek nod to what I looked like, in this delicate, flowery thing, felt promising. Telling, even. Like he actually enjoyed seeing me in these sets, too, something I couldn't always ascertain from his lack of commentary.

"Tell me I'm beautiful," I'd said on occasion. "Do you even like me in this? Does it ... do ... anything for you?"

Sometimes he'd laugh at this suggestion. "Do you think my boner is lying? Of course I'm attracted to you."

I had a friend tell me that, in lieu of physical compliments or affectionate words, to let my partner's body do the talking for him. I wanted that to be true or, at least, for it to be enough. After a lifetime of feeling invisible, a lifetime of feeling unworthy in a body that didn't meet traditional beauty standards, and a lifetime of inexperience, I craved that validation, a compliment, a word of attraction or affection.

But I was also new to this—both sex and relationships. There would be moments of such connection, moments where I'd remind myself this was more than I'd ever had, more than I'd ever expected. Surely, it would be enough.

It wasn't.

Chapter 22

HOUSTON, WE ARE A NO-GO FOR TAKEOFF

I don't need to tell you that being a woman is complicated. But trying birth control for the first time in your thirties? That was a whole new level of fuckery I had not seen coming. A month after we started dating, I researched birth control options. The women in my family were incredibly fertile. One of my sisters had a natural set of twins and a set of triplets. I wanted to batten down the hatches before I set off on my sexual misadventures.

I was terrified of getting pregnant and wanted, despite Grant's assurances that we could just use condoms, to take *every* precaution. I'd also dealt with heavy periods my whole life and, although I'd resisted my doctor's suggestions of birth control to help manage it, now seemed like a prime opportunity to wrap it all up in a nice sexually responsible little bow.

I told Grant I was getting an implant as a heads up. I'd read up on the potential side effects: mood swings, depression, weight gain, occasional tremors, etc. "If I'm not acting myself, and you notice, can you let me know?"

This felt like the mature thing to do. I did not often experience side effects from other medications. I didn't expect anything unusual with this choice. I decided on the arm implant because it seemed less invasive than an IUD and less trouble than birth control pills, but there was no way to determine how my body would react to any option until I was on it.

My doctor told me, "Figuring out what birth control works for you is sort of like buying jeans. You keep trying different ones until you find the one that suits you." That sounded normal, non-threatening, and manageable. I made an appointment for early March with dreams of being ready to go to pound town in no time.

I wish someone had reminded me that, just like trying on jeans, adjusting to birth control at any age is a fucking nightmare.

THE SIDE EFFECTS STARTED GRADUALLY. The first month or two my flow and cramps lessened. The only annoyance was that, instead of a fairly standard six-day cycle, my period turned into a month-long saga: 26 days of constant bleeding followed by a week off.

"You just have to wait it out," my doctor reassured me. "You'll need at least six months to fully adjust. This will pass."

In or out of a relationship, six months is a long time. It is especially long when you are in the fledgling stage of experimenting with your sexuality and you only have four to five days every month to *get it on* without it looking like a murder scene. Then you start to feel a light string of forewarned mood swings shift into full bouts of utter despair. Within a few months, it felt like my body was in total revolt. I sobbed on a few occasions when I realized that Grant and I wouldn't be seeing each other in the four-to-five-day window in question as the months progressed.

On the one hand, I was excited to have all these new physical and emotional experiences with him. On the other hand, being held hostage by my own biological schedule when I'd only tried to be prepared felt wickedly unfair. To top it off, I was told that if I removed the implant early, I would likely have to start the process all over again with a new option.

While my "always winter and never Christmas" periods continued to cramp my style and my emotional state darkened, I was determined to ride it out and see where we landed in September. I could live with that.

The tremors began a few months in. Anytime I started to feel anxious, it was like I lost my poker face. Any disquiet I was feeling manifested in trembling hands, shaking shoulders, neck twitches, or full-body spasms where my spine locked and my back arched like something out of a horror movie. I could be perfectly calm, curled up with him watching a movie, laying with my head on his chest as we talked long into the night, sitting next to him at church, or going out for dinner—unaware that I was nervous about anything at all. But when even the faintest tremor started in my fingers, my stomach would bottom out with dread.

The dread made it worse, always, as my own fear flooded my system in an adrenaline rush because there was no way to stop the tremors. All I could do was wait for them to run their course. Sometimes they would last just a few minutes, other times it might be hours, my spine arching, hands clenching, tears pouring down my face through ragged gasps. Sometimes they'd last even after I'd fallen asleep.

"You can breathe, right?" Grant asked once, holding me.

I'd twitch and shake and spasm, clinging to the arm he'd wrap around my waist, trying to let my breathing sync with his while my back pressed into his chest, his chin tucked into the side of my neck. "I can breathe," I'd say through chattering teeth, tears welling. "Just don't leave me, please? I'm sorry. *I'm sorry. I'm sorry.*" My words would get smaller, more pitiful, saturated with fear and crippling vulnerability. I'd never been seriously injured or sick before. I was unused to showing anyone this kind of weakness. The thought of facing them alone was worse than my embarrassment over needing him so desperately.

"Don't apologize," he'd always say. "I'm not going anywhere."

Once, he attempted to sleep in the guest room down the hall when he had to get up early for work the next day and the tremors wouldn't lessen over hours. I understood, but it still terrified me. Shaking, alone, in the dark, it felt like a vice had clamped down on my chest, my tears streaming, holding in a scream as I panicked and tried not to spasm harder. He came back before it got any worse.

There were times when he asked if he should call an ambulance. I begged him not to. Calling an ambulance felt like escalating this to a true emergency. That something was wrong with me. Every time, I'd beg him, "Don't leave me, *please* don't leave me."

He'd hold me tighter, his voice soothing. "I'm not going anywhere, I promise." Sometimes it felt like that promise was the only thing holding me together, and that I might shatter if he ever broke it.

"YOU'RE VERY SENSITIVE," my doctor said when I went—twice—to talk to her about my worsening reactions. "The hormones in your system must be feeding into your anxiety." By August, my never-ending periods had ceased, and I was beginning to hope that the tremors might, too. "You're having an extreme reaction," she continued, "but not an uncommon one. We can wait or switch it out for something new."

We were close to the six-month mark. The thought of starting from the beginning again felt daunting. I was willing to wait a little longer, even as Grant tried—and failed—to persuade me to have the implant removed.

It was hard to explain that birth control felt like the answer to not just avoiding pregnancy, but also managing my periods. My flow was much lighter—something I'd always wanted. My cramping had minimized. My cycle was coming back more regularly and it felt manageable for the first time, even as everything else teetered out of control. I was adamant to see it through and hoped the tremors would abate as well.

WE DEVELOPED a kind of rhythm when they continued into early fall. Grant's presence was a balm. If my hand started shaking in public, I'd slip my hand into his and hold on tight. If we were in bed, he'd pull me close, wrapping his arms around me or tracing patterns on my skin with his fingers—a sensation that, for whatever reason—always had an intensely calming effect. As the weeks passed, sometimes it felt like the tremors were lessening. Hours-long episodes faded to under an hour. They rarely happened when he wasn't around. He was tender and caring. It was a side of him I didn't often see outside of the episodes.

Grant was affectionate, but he rarely initiated touching me, rarely paid me any physical compliments, rarely showed any signs of physical or sexual attraction outside of sexual intercourse. With birth control wreaking havoc on my body, the opportunities for sex were rare. As months passed and our sex life slowed, it started to feel like Grant was mainly affectionate when comforting me during a tremoring episode. In some ways, his care when the tremors happened started to become addicting—which blossomed into a brand-new worry. "I sssssswear I'm not faking it," I'd stutter through chattering teeth.

I analyzed it over and over again. Was this something I could control? It didn't feel like it. The more I tried to "hold them in" or force myself to calm down, the worse my tremors got. Maybe my subconscious craved his undivided attention. Maybe it was all a plot to get the touch and affection I craved after a lifetime of living without it.

"You're not faking," he'd tell me, sometimes sternly, reminding me that sometimes I'd tremor beside him in my sleep.

"I'm sorrrrrry," I'd chatter again, agonized over the complete loss of control. "I'm sorry, I'm sorry, I'm sorry." My spine locked up. My hands clenched.

"I'm here, Allora." He'd reach for me. "I'm not going anywhere."

Chapter 23

ALLORA VS DEPRESSION

Depression crept in as the nights became longer. I understood what depression was. I'd seen its impact on other people in my life. But I had no idea how it would feel. It caught me off-guard. I didn't recognize the signs until I was standing hip-deep in despair too thick to crawl out of on my own.

I'm not saying I'd never been sad before or that my life has been without strife. I'd developed manageable anxiety in my mid-twenties, but depression slipped into my life slowly, quietly. Strings of listless, sleepless nights evolved into uncontrollable sobbing in the shower, to arguments with Grant that worsened when I realized I wasn't acting like myself. Disagreements, big or small, felt momentous. Monstrous. Ungainly. It felt like an undercurrent of discontent had entered the chat and, as the months trudged on, it worsened.

"You need therapy," Grant would tell me. "This isn't like you."

"I can't afford therapy," I'd snap. "I'm doing everything I can." No matter how he broached this subject, it always felt like he was saying I wasn't doing enough, or I that could try harder, do more. I think he was just overwhelmed and worried.

By October I'd given up on my birth control implant once I recognized how severely the side effects impacted my quality of life.

Then a brief, unsuccessful stint on the pill made my emotions plummet. I was also living on my own for the first time. Money was tight. I was on a strict budget and living paycheck to paycheck. As I racked up credit card debt to cover any house emergencies and other unexpected necessities, there was simply no money left for therapy co-pays.

"Ask your parents," he'd press. "They'll help. I know they will."

I knew they would, too, but I didn't want to ask. Life was getting back to normal, and all of us were pretending moving out and buying a house had been 100% my idea. I wanted to prove that I was thriving. The last thing I wanted to do was to come crawling back to ask for money, even for a mental health crisis. My pride, to my own detriment, wouldn't allow it. The shaking hadn't stopped, and I was told the side effects from birth control withdrawal could also be brutal.

"There's no shame in asking for help, Allora," Grant would say.

I couldn't accept that, and I was determined to prove to everyone that it was the right call.

I was unprepared for how low the lows could get. There were moments of agony I'd never known before or since. Moments of simply being *alive* felt excruciating. Forget the promise of brighter days ahead; I could barely survive the next few seconds, minutes, hours—let alone days. I'd cry and cry for hours, tremoring, clutching Grant if he was there, lying awake for brutal, sleepless nights if he wasn't.

I couldn't figure out what was missing. *What was wrong?* I felt like a black hole, my sadness swallowing up everything in its path. I had no idea how to fill the emptiness, how to make it stop. That realization was even worse. By all accounts, I should have been happy. Instead, I felt like I was drowning, and I had no idea which direction to swim up for air.

I'd been coming to the realization that it felt like my life had been building and building to this "high," if you will. I'd grown and changed so much in the last few years, to the point that my life was barely recognizable now from what it had been. But even if you reach the top of a mountain, there are always taller mountains to climb once you get there. I couldn't appreciate the journey or view.

I wondered, if I could flip my life upside down chasing my dreams and still end up unhappy, did that mean the struggle had been pointless? Did that mean I'd never be happy again?

A part of me knew this was the result of some mean, hormonal cocktail mixing with a season of extreme upheaval. By November, I was one month off birth control, but complete withdrawal would take months. When you find yourself staring sleeplessly into the night, unable to pass out on your strongest dose of anxiety meds, being told something might take months to change felt unbearable. I didn't know how to let Grant help. It felt like there was no way to avoid dragging him down my sadness hole, despite his assurances to the contrary.

I was emotionally weakened. Things that normally rolled right off my shoulders clung to me. Our arguments, mostly navigated without tears before, always left me in endless crying fits. As my inability to curb my emotions worsened, so did my tremors. Whenever Grant said something dumb, as boys occasionally do, I couldn't seem to avoid the hurt of even the most innocent misunderstandings.

Everything hurt.

"You're not the same person I met at the beginning of the year," Grant said, the warning shot for a fight that felt like it had come out of nowhere.

The night before we snuggled, been silly, and made out. I tucked my nose beneath his chin—inside the hollow of his neck. It was my favorite way to cuddle him, hug him. It was a feeling of fitting perfectly. We watched a movie and he'd held my hand, brushing his thumb over my knuckles.

Now we were sitting next to each other on my couch, our knees almost touching, but the distance was unbreachable. "My life has changed in every way possible," I'd fired back. "Of *course* I'm a different person." This declaration, although not untrue, only made me angrier. If anything, I was furious that my life had been upended and he expected sameness, while his had remained the same.

Grant leaned his head back against the couch and sighed deeply. "I need you to take this seriously and try to fix it. I can't fix it for you."

"And I'm not asking you to fix me," I replied. "I'm asking you to hug me, hold me, and tell me I'm pretty once in a while. *Can you do that?*"

The conversation went on for hours. After a tense two days of sidestepping potential arguments, I was exhausted. But, despite being asked several times, Grant wouldn't let it go. Was I aware that my depression and anxiety were a problem? Of course. But I also felt like I was doing everything I could and, after all, I was still living my life. I was still working, paying my bills, going to church, going to doctors, visiting my friends and family. I was still *living*. Any suggestion that I was not doing enough, when I felt like I could barely do it *at all*, felt like the biggest insult. Eventually, mid-conversation, one of my hands started to tremor.

Grant covered my hand with his, looking me full in the face as tears of frustration started to well in my eyes. "It's not that I care that you tremor, Allora. It's that I'm worried that you're *not* worried about why it's happening. They aren't going away."

I let him hug me. I was exhausted by my perpetual cloud of sadness. I didn't want to talk about this anymore, but I understood he was worried. In some ways, I was worried, too. I'd been to three different doctors. Medical bills were piling up. I was doing what I could, even if he didn't see that. It felt like a truce.

My anxiety didn't see it that way.

The next morning, I woke up in a panic. My defensiveness and frustration from the night before had calcified into an icy fear; Grant couldn't see that I was sad. I could no longer show him my sadness. I slipped out of bed before he woke up, showered, took Digory for a walk, did dishes, and made us breakfast.

He came down and tried to lighten the mood with a joke, but he only saw me stone-faced. He thought I was angry, when really I was trying to hold a panic attack at bay.

He was right; I *was* different. I was constantly sad. I didn't want to be this pathetic in front of him anymore. We tried to brush it off over breakfast, but it came up again in an argument that only continued to escalate. "I can't control this, and I'm doing the best I can," I said, anger creeping in as our tempers flared.

"You are the only one who can control this," he countered. "You are the only one who can change this. I can't do it for you."

"I'm not asking you to."

"Allora, you're not taking this *seriously*."

We went round and round in circles, my voice even, tone frigid, fingers gripping the edge of the table. I just wanted it to stop. His expression was flat, angry. I didn't understand what he wanted from me. Did he think therapy would just flip a happiness switch in my brain? Why couldn't he see I was trying my best and that I was hurt because I thought I could lean on him?

I could not see his worry through our anger.

I'd had enough. "We can decide, right now, how the rest of this day is going to be," I snapped. "We can take a time out, cuddle, maybe do some decorating. I don't know. But if you are telling me that you cannot be with me while I am figuring this out, you should just break up with me right now." I got up, cleared our dishes, and set them in the sink. It allowed us both a few seconds to catch our breath and calm down.

When I sat back down, his body was rigid, expression cold. "What if I say something and you just misconstrue it again?"

"Then I will ask you what you meant so I understand and don't assume the worst of you."

"Allora, you overthink everything I say. Every word."

"Maybe. But I always ask for clarification so that it doesn't get the better of me. I don't make hasty assumptions."

Despite both of our intentions, this moment was only getting worse. I stepped back into the kitchen, began cleaning dishes, and he headed upstairs. Within a few minutes I got a text.

I'm leaving. I need space.

My rib cage crumpled. He couldn't be serious. We had argued before, but we always worked it out. He'd never threatened to leave before.

I wish you would take alone time, but please don't leave, I texted back.

My skin felt cold. I waited ten minutes, then went upstairs to talk it out. He refused to look at me. At one point, he asked me to get out of the way as he angrily got dressed and packed his things. Bewildered and sliding into pure panic, I went back downstairs and waited for him on the couch. Surely, we could still turn this around. He wouldn't actually leave, not like this. Not in the middle of this. I couldn't think of anything more hurtful.

He came down the stairs, suitcase in hand. He didn't look at me as he brushed past me for the front door. "There's no way to sugarcoat this," he said evenly. "I'm leaving." He was gone in seconds.

I couldn't stop staring. The sight of him walking away, from me, down my driveway. Not turning around. Not saying goodbye. Just nothing. The black hole in my chest expanded.

I was breaking. Broken.

I fell apart.

I CALLED MY BEST FRIEND, sobbing, tremoring. "He … he left." I said between gasps. "He left me."

She didn't ask questions. She was at my house in fifteen minutes, holding me as I sobbed into her lap. No one besides Grant had ever seen me tremor before. I couldn't stop them as my spine locked, and I spasmed in her arms.

"Allora—Allora, *can you breathe?*"

I nodded. I couldn't stop crying, couldn't stop seeing him walking away. She stayed until I was calm and made me a frothy cup of hot chocolate. We cuddled and watched *Little Women* (the 90s version, obviously). He texted me. I couldn't bring myself to read it.

"Do you want me to read it first?" She rubbed my back.

I shook my head. "No … no. I just want to try not thinking about it for a while." I couldn't hold the pieces of me together. She left after I took my anxiety meds and crawled into bed. When I finally worked up the nerve to open his messages—sent one after the other—they crushed me.

I no longer feel safe at your house. I will not come back until you get help.

What could he possibly mean? Had I been angry? Of course.

But how could I have made him feel unsafe? I hadn't even raised my voice, hadn't done anything but sit stock-still across from him. Didn't he see I was trying? That I was doing everything I could? But what stops a fucking black hole? How could *anything* stop this?

We volleyed texts back and forth at first. Then I went quiet, desperate for my meds to kick in and to drift off to sleep. He torpedo-texted my phone after a few hours, threatening to call my mom if I didn't let him know I was okay. He said I was out of line, slamming plates and doors, but we could get through this. I was, again, bewildered. Slammed *what*? Did *what*? He was painting a picture of something that didn't happen. Was he even seeing me? Was he seeing an old fight with an ex? I didn't know.

All I could think was that he left me. He promised not to.

You left me. You know that was my biggest fear. There is no us. I'm not yours to worry about anymore.

Are you breaking up with me? He fired back.

My chest tightened. I didn't want to say yes, but that's what was happening. *You left.* I texted. *And you're not sorry about it. You could have taken a walk, could have left and come back, but you left. At my lowest point. You walked away, and you didn't come back.*

How could things just end like this? he said. *Why are you not listening? I want to help you. Let me help you.*

I didn't answer any of the other texts that came through that night. Some worried, some unintentionally cruel. I called my mom, gasping for deep breaths.

"Don't let him do this to you, Allora," my mom said. "Do you need me to call one of the girls? Can you be alone right now?"

I realized I was scaring her. I didn't know how to stop it. "I'm just going to go to sleep," I promised. "I'll be okay."

"Don't open any more texts, Allora. Things will be better in the morning."

Morning? Morning felt like a millennium away. How do you survive through those next seconds, minutes, of pure agony? I couldn't get enough air. Couldn't stop crying. My skin ached where it met my sheets. The pressure of the mattress against my body felt like rocks against an open wound. Everything felt too hot, too cold, too hard, and there was no relief. There was nothing I could do to stop the pain shredding through me in waves. Nothing to be done … and I was all alone.

He'd left. He'd left *me*.

He left.

I KNEW Grant had been overwhelmed. Scared, even. Hell, I'd been scared, too. I'd never felt so out of control with my emotions. It felt like there had been no bottom to my despair. This was a version of me that he never signed up for. I couldn't help but feel like there should have been another way to try to help without breaking me. When I tried to defend him to my mother, she hugged me and said, "Allora, if he was so worried, then why did he leave?"

I didn't have an answer.

Grant immediately wanted to mend things. He believed the fight we had was just that—a fight. But there was a moment in time when we'd both looked at our relationship, and both of us had no intention of continuing it. To me, that was more.

I'd said, "There is no us."

He'd said, "I'm done."

It didn't matter that the next day he wanted to fix things. He asked me if I wanted to, too. Breaking up felt like breaking apart. It felt like him leaving over and over again—the moment I'd watched him walk down the driveway without looking back. Staying together? That felt like hope being sucked slowly, but persistently, out of me. We loved each other, didn't we? How could two people who loved each other hurt each other so badly?

How did you put that all aside and start again?

Did I even want to?

WE DIDN'T SEE each other for another week. We were supposed to be doing Thanksgiving at my family's house, but I didn't want to see him. Showing up alone was brutal. No one said anything about my breakdown. Everyone acted like everything was normal. No one asked about Grant or commented on my red-rimmed eyes or trembling hands. They gave me big hugs and pretended nothing was wrong. I had been so excited for him to be there with me; now I couldn't even say his name. I had trusted him, let him see the darkest, most vulnerable side of me, and he walked away.

After, all I could think about was how I'd never tuck my nose beneath his chin again. I'd never feel the inside of that hollow while he hugged me tight. I'd never hold his hand again.

THE FOLLOWING weekend he suggested meeting up in a neutral place, a local café. He suggested, too, that we give each other a big hug when we saw each other again—the first time since this fight.

We aren't strangers, we shouldn't act like it, he texted. *We should say everything we mean with that hug.*

But what did I mean? I was anxious. It took all my nerve to walk up to the café door. Warm light spilled out to the darkened rain-slick streets beyond. I saw him waiting inside, tea in hand, before I opened the door. I felt hard. Cold. I did not come here to be comforted—I came here to seek some kind of justice, maybe understanding. I would not be soft or kind. I would be direct.

He looked handsome—his hair crisply shorn on the sides, styled well. He'd trimmed his beard. He was wearing his favorite sherpa over a white Henley, new dark jeans, his favorite Timberland boots —almost the same outfit he'd sported on our first date.

He came right up to me, arms open. I was stiff, unyielding, and, in answer, my hands locked up as the first round of tremors washed over me. They'd never been so strong in public before. Embarrassed, my cheeks flushed. I tried to hug him back. I was appalled by the wave of relief that washed over me. I thought I'd never feel this again. Was I weak for melting into him so quickly?

"Let's go outside for a minute," he said. "Less people."

I pulled back from the hug, grateful for the burst of cool air, despite the rain, as we stepped out the door. I hugged him again, this time holding on. How could a hug say, *"You hurt me"* and *"I want to forgive you, but I don't know how to trust you again*"? My spine started locking up.

"It's okay." He rubbed my back. "You're okay. Thank you for coming."

I wanted his comfort, had relied on it before, but I also resented it. He'd been my safe space. I'd given him all my love and trust. He'd crushed me.

I wore all black: black pants, a high-neck black top that squared off my shoulders into hard lines, a black faux leather jacket, black boots. I once described myself as a "fucking ray of sunshine." Right now, I didn't have much left. But I was determined, in this moment, to share none with him.

He guided us inside to a quiet corner with two worn couches so we could sit facing each other. He said he was sorry. He had no idea leaving would affect me that way. He said he wanted to be there for me. He understood I was doing my best. He wanted this to work. All his friends and family thought the world of me.

I was unrelenting. Fire and brimstone. I had never been so *angry* before. "I'm not surprised your friends and family like me, Grant. I work hard at it. I'm likable, I'm accomplished. I have accomplished a lot with my life." My hands were shaking. I let them. I wanted him to see how this impacted me. My neck locked up, my chin twitching to the right. *Oh goody, that's a new one.*

I held his gaze. I had spent many years feeling inadequate. I was thrilled by my rage, my confidence. How I believed my own words. "I want us to try again, but I don't know if I trust you anymore. I give trust freely, but it's hard to earn back once it's broken."

He asked me if we could try again.

Hesitantly, I said yes.

HE WALKED me to my car. I couldn't control the tremor in my hands when he hugged me goodbye. I felt drained. My anger spent. I'd said what I needed to say and now felt empty. This was not love or trust, not like there had been. Maybe there was understanding.

He wanted to be there for me. I was afraid to let him.

I was afraid to trust him, or to potentially reawaken that all-consuming agony of not wanting to spend another conscious second in my body. The pain of that was fresh. I felt like I was trying to piece together shattered glass with too many pieces of tape. I wanted to give him a second chance, had agreed to give him a second chance, but I was also afraid of what that second chance entailed. Something had changed.

Still, I tucked my nose in against his neck. I let him hold me even when I couldn't make my hands loosen to hold him back.

"Can I kiss you on the cheek?" he asked.

It did not feel like enough of a promise, after all of this. I was desperate to reconnect. I tilted my head up, pressing my lips to his as tremors raced down my spine. I didn't feel less empty, but maybe the emptiness was making way for openness. Maybe that was enough to start.

All I knew is that I would either marry this man or he would break my heart.

I STARTED THERAPY THAT MONTH. My parents covered the cost like I knew they would if I'd asked sooner. I met with a therapist weekly through the holidays, catching her up on the lore of my life, letting her see the cracks and broken pieces. It felt like a joke, honestly, filling her in on the events of the last year and giving the context of my history, my family, and my relationship.

"You don't have to keep defending everyone," she told me. "You can say how you feel without explaining why they said or did something."

Could I?

I was willing to do whatever I could to feel like me again. But more worryingly, what I didn't understand was how talking to her would help. And, worse, what if nothing helped?

What if I was just like this … forever?

How was I supposed to find me again?

Chapter 24

"I FEEL LIKE CONFETTI."

By December, I was a husk. I felt so far from the girl that had started off 2023, that happy ray of sunshine. Between struggling with birth control withdrawal, depression, living alone for the first time, and now this fight with Grant, I was desperate to lean into the magic and nostalgia of the holiday season. During the emotional after-shocks of the fight, I wanted for it all to wash away somehow, for it all to not be hard anymore, for it all to be sweet and simple.

That's a lot of pressure to put on one holiday season, but here we were. Despite everything, I wanted to make memories in my own little house. I asked Grant if he would spend Christmas Eve with me, stay the night, have our own Christmas morning, host his parents for brunch, and then go to my parents'. This meant, for the first time in my life, I was not going to be with my family on Christmas morning. Of course, I had many big feelings about that. But this year had been different, and it made sense that some of my holiday traditions would be different too.

Christmas Eve arrived. We planned to go to Mass with my family where one of my sisters was cantoring. Then we'd have a quiet evening alone. Your girl looked fly in a retro-style chiffon, red plaid blouse, accented with a little black neck tie, paired with a black, high-waisted suspender skirt. I wore my hair up in a high ponytail, spiraled into one single curl, with a red lip. I finished it all off with a black pair of heeled Mary Janes.

I waited in the dining room as Grant finished getting ready. My hands folded behind my back, head titled as I waited for him to come down the stairs.

Once he cleared the last step, he spied me, paused, and smiled. "You look awesome." He looked me up and down.

I smiled back, cheeks heating, feeling pretty and girlish and *me*. It felt like a promise of more, something like hope or possibility. "Thanks." I did a little twirl. "Do you see my hair, too?"

"I see your hair, too. And yes, you look very, very cute."

I beamed as we got in my car and headed for church. Grant suggested we go back and forth requesting Christmas songs to listen to for the hour-long drive. I started off with some of my traditional favs and some funny ones like Straight No Chaser's, "12 Days of Christmas." He surprised me with ones I had never heard before, like the *South Park* Christmas Special songs. I am not a *South Park* girly, but we were having a good time. It was cold, dark, and a little bit icy as we crested the steps and slipped inside the church.

This was an old-school Catholic church. There was beautiful artwork on the walls, giant stained-glass windows, white string lights everywhere, big Christmas trees behind the altar, wreaths hung on all the pews. The glow from the lights was warm and soft. The church was packed.

I spied my parents and siblings towards the front. They'd saved a spot for us at the end of the pew. There was something about that, slipping in beside my family, Grant with me, that lit me up inside.

He reached over and shook my father's hand.

Mass began as my sister walked up to the altar to sing. We all stood.

This moment meant the world to me. I'd been squished into a pew with my massive family on Sundays for my entire life, but I'd never been squished in a pew with a boyfriend. It all overwhelmed me—the feel of him at my side, my sister's stunning voice, the Christmas lights, and all the families with kids. After a lifetime alone, experiencing family traditions with a partner had always felt impossibly distant—a faraway dream forever out of reach. I hadn't realized till then how much I'd always wanted this.

My left hand started to tremor. As it started shaking, Grant slipped his hand in mine and squeezed. It was a small, almost invisible moment. But that quiet support, that lending of strength, the knowledge that he was there with me, felt like an almost painful swell of hope.

After the service, we headed over to my sister's house. She'd made our family's signature sauce with fresh pasta and meatballs for dinner, and her house was decked out in cozy, Christmas finery. Despite almost dating for a year, I hadn't brought Grant around to that many family events. Watching him make conversation with my parents and playing with my niece and my nephews—all of it felt like a potent mix of everything I'd ever wanted.

Once we got back home, I was determined to lean into all the cuteness I could muster. I'd gotten me and Grant matching pajama pants. I'd never had silly, cutesy holiday moments with a partner. I recognized them, relished them, didn't want to ever let them go. I could barely contain my excitement as we sat on the couch to exchange Christmas cards (saving gifts for morning). I'd challenged us both to reflect on what the year together had meant to us. After a year of collecting firsts with someone who meant so much to me, Grant decided to surprise me with one more. I'd told him that I had never slow danced with anyone other than my dad. Homeschooled, right? I never had a prom.

After we exchanged cards, Grant looked over at me and cleared his throat. "So, how would you feel about having a slow dance right now?"

My answering smile had serious wattage behind it. "I feel pretty good about that, actually."

We stood up in our matching pajama pants. My little Christmas tree in the corner cast a soft glow. I hadn't known we were going to slow dance ahead of time, but I knew exactly what song I wanted if the opportunity ever arose: "Fly Me to the Moon" by Tony Bennett.

Grant extended his hands. "You know, there's a couple of ways you can slow dance." He showed me, guiding my hands. "You can put your hand here, I can put my hand here, or we can hold hands. Or there's the way where you can put both your arms around my neck, and I can put both my arms around your waist."

I swallowed hard. "That all sounds perfect."

He took my hand and slid his other around my waist. "You can lean your head on my shoulder, if you want."

We swayed around my dining room, the floorboards creaking beneath us as Tony Bennett crooned.

I looked into his face as tears welled in my eyes. "You know, if you have the opportunity to love me for my whole life, I think I will request a slow dance every Christmas Eve."

I'll never forget the wry smile on his face, the way he turned his head towards me to nod. "I think that can be arranged."

"I know I'm crying," I whispered, "but I feel so *happy*. Like, I'm full of confetti, and I could just burst."

It felt like magic, like everything good and right was possible in the world. It felt like joy. After months of soul-crushing doubt and fear, far from feeling safe and good about the decisions I'd made that year, he just hugged me. Right then, it was everything I ever wanted. When we went to bed on my first Christmas Eve *not* alone, we cuddled until we fell asleep.

Chapter 25

WHEN YOU START TO REALIZE YOU DON'T FIT

"We're so good at dating," I told Grant on our first date. It became a running gag in those first few months—something we'd pat ourselves on the back for as we "excelled" at communication. I'd grown up ignoring or holding in things that bothered me for the sake of keeping the peace. But keeping hurt inside eats away at you. It burns holes in your chest.

I was determined to go about dating in a different way when I met Grant. If I had a thought—any worry—where the two of us were involved, I challenged myself to say it. I developed a personal rule that the harder a thing was to say, the more important it was to say it. I wanted to air out what bothered me as it happened. I wanted nothing to fester. We had this. We loved each other. And because we loved each other, because we were communicating, because I was fighting to shape a future together with every fiber of my being, I thought that would be enough.

"You make my life better, Allora," Grant told me as we drove through swatches of sunshine

I was driving, picking him up for a long weekend together.

He'd launched into another topic.

I don't know if he realized that I hadn't replied. I looked across at him. A realization crept up my spine with prickly tendrils: *my life is harder with you in it.* If that were true, what did it mean? Were we unravelling? Was I? It made other moments between us come into sharper focus, and I wasn't sure I wanted to know where this realization led.

AFTER A HAUNTED HAYRIDE together on Friday the 13th, Grant got COVID. We agreed he'd stay with me in quarantine so he wouldn't put his senior parents at risk. By the end of the week, I'd gotten it, too. Neither of us had gotten COVID before, and, to top it off, it was the most uninterrupted time we'd ever spent together.

I was 100% ready to play the part of nurse, dolling out meds, making soup, helping in whatever way I could. I was not prepared to go a week with the small annoyances of living with a partner— the toilet seat never being put down, picking up after someone, existing in a space with someone without spending quality time with them. To top it off, my shower plumbing burst—flooding my kitchen—which meant I didn't have a functioning shower for the entirety of the week.

By week's end, I was at an emotional breaking point with stress and being the absolute sickest I'd ever been. I couldn't breathe, couldn't think, and when one thing after another set off some of Grant's OCD triggers, we decided the best thing would be for him to go home and shower since he was feeling better.

"But you'll be back later tonight, right?" I asked.

He hesitated. "I ... I have to go, Allora. There are things that need to happen for my OCD to calm down. And you're too sick to help."

"Just tell me what to do, and I'll do it," I whispered, head heavy and lolling against the couch. "I can help."

"You're sick," he responded gently. "I can't ask that of you, I'll be back as soon as I can." It did not register that he wasn't coming back till later that night. My fever raged, and existing felt *so* hard. He called to check in on me, told me he'd be back in the morning, and that's when it sunk in.

"You're leaving me? *Alone?*" After a week of taking care of him, it seemed impossible. He wouldn't do that to me. Couldn't. He *promised* not to. It didn't matter how he tried to explain it. Choking on my tears, I slid into a panic attack. Dragging myself off the couch, I found a bottle of Lysol wipes and started cleaning every surface I could find, trailing used wipes on the floor as I went. I'd make this house spotless—germ free—so long as he came back. If he only wouldn't leave me alone. *He couldn't possibly leave me alone.*

I cried so hard I threw up and, on my hands and, I cleaned that up, too. He texted to check in on me again.

I'm all alone, I texted back. *I just want my mom.*

I knew, no matter how good the reason was, no one—least of all my parents—would understand if I told them I'd been there for him all week, but he'd left me the moment I got sick. I understood Grant's OCD triggers. I understood this was all a case of cosmically bad timing, but all I wanted was for someone to take care of me. To not leave me alone like this.

I crawled back onto the couch, wheezing, tremoring, and cried myself to sleep. I woke up to a hand on my shoulder, a gentle touch. I blinked awake, gazing up at him. It was still dark, all the lights off except the dull glow outlining his face from the stairs behind us.

"You came back?" I rasped. Tears welled in my eyes.

He sighed. "I came back. Come on, let's get you up to bed."

He helped me up the stairs and tucked me into bed.

I laid on my side, clutching him, as he slipped under the covers beside me. He pulled me to his chest once. "You came back."

"I came back," he said quietly. "I'm not going anywhere."

I fell asleep against him, but a new fear blossomed across my chest.

GRANT STAYED a few days longer to make sure I was okay. It had been a long, tense two weeks. My emotions were all in a tangle. All I could think of was: *are we bad for each other?*

If two well-meaning people could cause each other such hurt and pain, then did we even belong together? Was I sacrificing a better future because I didn't have enough courage to let go of this one? I couldn't dispel my growing disquiet. It was a knotted, roiling thing.

One night, snuggled up in the dark, we shouldn't have been talking about serious things after the past week, but there we were anyway. I felt us tiptoe into a topic that made my stomach twist. I rolled away from him, onto my back, my spine starting to tense—an indication that the tremors were coming. I reached for his hand, squeezing, as my teeth began chattering. I could almost feel the spot where my anxiety sat, a potent concentration of dread and nerves. It felt like I could press down on it when I placed my hand below my breasts, thumb pressing on my sternum.

He started chatting again, asking me silly questions, anything to distract me from panicking.

"I appreciate what you're doing," I told him. They lasted for a few seconds at a time, seizing my whole body, before tapering off briefly and starting again. "Distracting me."

"Is that what I'm doing?" he teased.

"I have a silly question," I replied. "I—" I paused. It felt stupid to say it out loud. My face heated. "It's not exactly even a question it's …" I couldn't bear how vulnerable it sounded. Even though we were lying beside each other, shoulder to shoulder in the dark, hands clasped, this question felt like too much. Technically, we hadn't even known each other for a full year yet. We'd made no "in sickness and in health" vows. We'd been starting to rely on each other, but all of it still felt like unknown territory.

"Well now you have to say it," he prodded.

"It's silly … you're going to think it's silly."

He waited.

I sighed. "I've been holding my hand right here—where I can feel my anxiety." I paused, cheeks heating. "I was wondering what it would feel like if you pressed down there. I know it's silly."

"It's not silly. It makes a lot of sense, actually, with how you express yourself. Your sexuality. Your love languages." He turned on his side to face me. I couldn't read his expression as his hand dipped to my lower stomach, feeling for the hem of my shirt. His fingers brushed my own, grazing the side of my breast.

"But this isn't going anywhere tonight," he warned, direct as ever.

I rolled my eyes. "Not *everything* is about sex." I shifted his touch to the spot above my sternum, right where I could feel all my nerves churning. When he pushed down, even lightly, I felt like I could breathe. I took in deep, slow breaths as he pressed his forehead to mine. I moved my free hand to the back of his neck, where my fingers tangled in his hair. We waited like that—breathing quietly in the dark.

"You can let go," I told him after a few minutes; I didn't want him to.

"I want to stay here longer." He waited a beat. "You can ask anyone; not many people get moments like this, Allora."

I snorted. "Don't ruin the magic of this, Grant." My heart thundered in my chest. "You know I'm not swayed by crowd approval—only by what feels right."

This felt right, didn't it? Like he was capable of being exactly who I needed him to be. My worries dissipated with every breath: was he enough? Was I too needy? Was I sacrificing too much? I couldn't figure out if I was just never satisfied, or if some part of me knew this wasn't enough and I needed more.

"Thank you," I said on an exhale. "I *missed* you."

We'd been sick, fragile, co-existing. I had missed connecting with him. I turned and kissed his forehead, the first I'd given him after a week of illness and misery.

He kissed my cheek and laid back down. I tucked myself against his shoulder. I didn't remember falling asleep, but I was tangled up with him when I woke up.

"WE'RE LIKE POETRY BEING WRITTEN," Grant told me once. He'd wondered if it was corny.

I didn't think so. Most of the poetry I knew was sad. I wondered if that meant we were doomed.

It felt like there were two parts of me at war with each other. There was genuine love here. I'd never felt like this with anyone else. I knew he'd become the most important person in the world to me. But there was this other feeling, something insistent that kept creeping in: that I was making myself smaller for us to work. I'd been consumed, over the course of our relationship, with the question of whether I was good enough, or too much, or not enough for him. I hadn't stopped myself to ask: was he right for me?

THINKING about breaking up felt like waking up to realize your favorite shirt no longer fit. Whether it's your body naturally changing, or the shirt itself shrank in the wash, you start to recognize the space the relationship has taken up in your life. The places where the material has become stretched or threadbare, or where your skin now chafes beneath it. You loved this person. You put your whole heart into creating and maintaining this connection.

Now what?

I dreamed my whole life of having someone to love and who loved me. Someone who was my person. Maybe this was all I needed. After all, being a version of myself who wasn't quite sure wasn't worse than being alone … right? I'd been alone. This was lightyears better than where I'd been before … right? Those questions gnawed at me as winter crept in. One night, I sat by the hearth at the family homestead with my mother, explaining how I wasn't feeling myself and how I wasn't sure what to do about it.

She looked up at me from the comforting glow of the fire. "You have a great job, your own home, your creativity, a little dog who loves you, a good car, a boyfriend. You could say that you have everything you've ever wanted. So why aren't you happy?"

That was the real question, wasn't it? Why wasn't I happy?

What was I missing?

EVEN THOUGH GRANT apologized after our next massive fight in November, everything started to change. I had approached our relationship with an open heart. I'd been determined to be my most honest, authentic self. I knew I wasn't perfect, but I'd changed, when I'd been so sure that nothing could ever change that about me. The COVID incident and the November fight had shaken my trust. Without that trust in him, in us, and in myself, other aspects of our relationship came into sharper focus. I didn't like the "me" I saw as a result.

Fights we'd had in the past resurfaced with new context. The lens of *"I've spent so much time getting to know this person. To love this person,"* had been replaced with, *"Does this person even know me at all?"* Because, why then, could they act this way? Say those things? Why did it feel like I'd changed so much about myself to make us fit when, maybe, we just didn't?

Promises that had been made and broken time and time again carried new weight. I'd been questioning since the beginning if he'd been ready to date me when mentions of his ex came up at least once every single time we saw each other.

At first, I encouraged him to talk about his past. I wanted to help in whatever way I could with him putting it behind him. As the months wore on, his ex didn't seem like a part of his past. She felt like a phantom, haunting us every time he mentioned her. Even if it was a complimentary remark, explaining how I was different or better than her, her name was still on his lips. Her presence was a constant. We'd fight. He'd promise to stop. She'd be mentioned again … and again … and again.

I never thought he was doing it to be cruel. He couldn't help it. It was a part of the way he told his stories to give context. But the more she was brought up, the less I felt seen. During our six month and one year anniversary dinners—occasions where we dressed up and went out to eat, the thing I remember the most is that, even when prompted, Grant couldn't think of a single question to ask me.

But he mentioned his ex at least twice each time.

There were moments I'd question if Grant was capable of dreaming as big as I was. I'd been in a constant state of growth and change over the last year, but he seemed to be content remaining exactly the same. Not that you should date someone expecting them to change, but I had changed in good ways and bad. I'd changed to make room for the life I wanted. I'd changed to be someone right for him. But there were some changes I wasn't willing to make, some dreams I didn't want to let go of or make smaller.

One night, late, when we'd driven through Burger King to pick up dinner, I told him how I wanted us to go down to Delaware together. My parents had a house near the beach there, and it was an inexpensive opportunity to travel.

Grant shook his head. "I just don't like doing all that driving like you and your family does. All the time in the car is uncomfortable."

I was taken aback. Besides our trip to New York City, we hadn't gone anywhere. I loved to travel—I couldn't wait to travel *with* him. In that moment, I realized: *you are comfortable with your world being small. With a quiet, cozy life. But I'm not.*

There is a part of me that wanted that kind of life, too, but I also wanted more. Much more. The feeling of "not fitting" started deepening from there, unraveling what we were and tangling in the sweetness of what we had been as the holiday season bled into the new year. I couldn't seem to let it go—the thought that we "didn't fit." He was wildly supportive, fully content to be in my corner as I burned with my own hopes, dreams, and goals. He wanted to be there for me. He was, in many ways, there for me when I needed him to be. But there had been moments when he hadn't been, and trust—once lost—was hard to rebuild.

"YOU'VE CHANGED," he said as we started fighting more and more. Without a sense of trust pulling us together, it became increasingly clear that we were no longer a safe space to admit big feelings or hard truths. "You're overthinking," he'd say. "You promised not to misinterpret what I say. You're breaking your word."

I'd reel from that. "I can't promise not to misinterpret what you say. That's impossible. I can do my best to be honest about how something I hear makes me feel. To go to you and seek clarity. But you don't get a blanket pass to just say whatever you want and expect me not to be hurt or react to it."

Sex, our one, strongest connection, got pulled into the maelstrom, too. I loved having sex with him, but my enthusiasm and eagerness began to sour as that, too, became a battlefield. We'd plan on having sex on certain days—a compromise, since my sex drive was higher than his—and the time would come and because of a fight or a stressor, or a date we'd planned running too long, sex would be cancelled or postponed. It became a quagmire of hurt as I craved intimacy—an indicator that we were okay. One way or another, it kept getting tossed aside.

"Can't we just cuddle or kiss?" he'd ask. "Those are forms of intimacy, too."

Yes, of course they were. I loved doing those things too. But sex, for me, was validating, powerful, connective. Without it, our fights stung more. The distance between us widened. As time wore on, the little cuts from those disagreements and disappointments deepened. Festered. Without sex, without feeling seen, without my big dreams, without any kind of physical validation, I couldn't help but wonder: *what am I fighting so hard to hold onto?*

Did he even like me—let alone love me?

This wasn't love. This couldn't be love. I knew it wasn't fair to either of us to keep something going that I could see was doomed. How do you realize you are no longer in love with the first person you've ever truly loved? How do you just … end?

I knew I had to, but I also couldn't figure out how I possibly could.

It ate me alive.

Chapter 26

CHOOSE YOUR HARD

You never know when something is going to be the last time. The thing I've learned about breakups is that you don't always see them coming. They can happen slowly, even if you know it's what you need while you're grasping for a reason to stay. They can still happen sandwiched between "I love yous." They can happen as you realize you are drifting apart and that you want different things out of life. They can happen when you started off as friends, but the longer you stay together, the warmth between you chills.

Breakups are an unmaking. Even though I thought about it for months, I still didn't see it coming. More accurately, I saw it coming and wished I hadn't. It felt like being told to evacuate for a hurricane, and I wasn't ready to leave until the house was already six feet underwater. Neither of us were horrible people doing horrible things to each other, but we couldn't stop hurting each other either.

I didn't wake up planning to break up with Grant the day that it happened. It was a normal day—we messaged each other sweet things. An argument escalated, a fight we'd had over and over again. It hit me midway through when we angrily hung up, each fuming at the other, that despite all our efforts, despite many conversations about things needing to change, nothing was changing. It was a cycle of hurt we couldn't escape. I said I thought we needed to break up and gave a few important reasons why. He asked that we take time to have space from each other, to really think this through. We stopped talking for two weeks—the longest we'd been quiet since we'd met a year ago.

It crushed me to answer the phone after those two weeks ended. He was excited to make another go of it, full of eager intent and promises of change. But I knew, before he even started talking, that this chapter of our lives was over. I'd spent a year getting to know him in a way I'd never known anyone before. In the end, he hadn't been ready to know and care about me in the same way. I was tired of fighting alone for us.

It was time to end. Choosing to walk away from something that wasn't bad, but wasn't what I needed, felt selfish. It felt like denying every good thing that happened between us. It didn't seem like the pain it caused could possibly be worth it. I grieved the connection that was now severed. There was the unmaking of all we had become to each other. There was the loss of little things, like knowing we'd never talk to each other the same way again, cuddle again, kiss again. I fixated on never being able to tuck my nose beneath his chin. I dreaded relearning how to be alone. I had gotten used to having someone to hold me at night, someone to call every day, someone who was my person in good times and in bad.

I drove to his house after another difficult phone call where we both struggled to come to terms with the fact that this was ending. I was crying, he was crying, and I desperately wanted to take this away from us. Despite all the hurt in the end, surely this couldn't be worth it. This pain couldn't be the right decision. He sat in my car as we walked for what felt like hours. At one point, I reached over to give him a hug.

He pulled back, tears in his wide eyes. "This is a 'goodbye forever' hug. I don't want a goodbye hug."

It wasn't a goodbye hug. It was a "I'm hurting, too," hug. It was a "I wish things could be different," hug. It was a "I wish you had been able to love me like I needed you to" hug. It was a "You were the first person to ever love me hug." A "I wish this didn't hurt so bad" hug.

It felt like being cleaved in two—impossible to survive.

Even a not-all-bad thing can be not good for you.

Chapter 27

DON'T LOOK BACK

The emotional impact of a breakup hit me like a tsunami—obliterating everything in its path in a massive wave. It was a decision I'd seen coming for a long time, but it didn't make living with the consequences any easier. Even with all the warning signs, fights, and hard conversations, the breakup hit Grant unexpectedly.

For me, shouldering Grant's pain, in addition to my own, felt unbearable. Even though I knew, deep down, that I'd made the right decision, it didn't seem possible that I had. How could something be right when it was hurting us both so badly? Was my own happiness worth this if the cost was someone else's pain? I couldn't believe how unworthy I felt of that reality. I'd hoped that a breakup would happen gently, lovingly. That, somehow, it could sting less, the blow could be softened. It was not.

Loneliness blindsided me. In the seconds, minutes, hours that followed, the thought of letting go felt impossible. How could we go from talking every day, long weekends together, occasional adventures or days out, telling each other every pain, joy, sorrow, and secret to nothingness? The unmaking of it all was overwhelming.

I surrounded myself with friends and family, leaving my house after work each day to visit someone as if I could outrun the sadness haunting my own home. Grant had spent the most time with me there. He'd made the adjustment period of living alone bearable. Now it felt like I could see him everywhere, the litany of memories a constant thrum. Part of me wanted to slam the door on all of them, block out every moment we'd spent together if it meant stopping the hurt. At the same time, severing the link between us seemed too painful.

Everywhere I turned, the people in my life, including my therapist, all recommended going no contact. Grant countered that we didn't need to, that we could still be there for each other, that we could limit our contact to every three days or so. I agreed. This felt like a temporary solution. This felt like he, too, still wanted to hold on to whatever goodness existed between us—however strained it may be.

I wrote myself a list detailing every reason I felt the breakup needed to happen and, upon each reread, the evidence seemed simple and clear. No one was the bad guy. We just didn't fit. I hadn't realized not fitting could hurt so much. Seeing it in writing helped. It was a clear ray of reason in a sea of churning pain, guilt, and grief. I could point to it and say, "See? You did everything you could to make this work."

WHEN I TOLD Grant about the list, he asked to see it. I thought it would help him understand my decision or, at least, give him closure. I'm still not sure if it was the right call.

A week after the breakup, sad conversations throughout, Grant texted me and asked if he could come over. He'd gotten into a big fight with someone, and he wanted to be in a safe, welcoming space. "I have other people I could call just … you were always who I used to call first. Is it okay if I come over? Sleep on your couch?"

The relief of seeing him again overwhelmed me. There had been a time where he'd been my safe space, too. Even though it was already 9 p.m. on a Saturday, I told him he could stay in the guest room—down the hall from my bedroom. It felt weird to say and even weirder to explain. It had only been a few weeks ago that we were curling up in each other's arms at night. There was a new distance now, a new wariness that was warranted, but unfamiliar.

By the time he walked through my door, I'd mustered the courage to make this as chill as possible, and I welcomed him with a big hug. I was startled that, after weeks of pain and ugliness, I still fit perfectly when I wrapped my arms around him, tucking my nose into the hallow beneath his chin. "Feel free to get cleaned up. I'm going to take Digory for a walk."

He nodded, emotionally wrung out. He seemed embarrassed that he called me at all. He didn't have to be. I didn't need to say yes; I wanted to. I missed our familiarity. It had taken too many hits to survive in the end, but I missed the echoes of it, even in this odd truce. Grant climbed the stairs as I headed out with Digory. It was late March, right before Easter. The crisp, early spring air was calming. I'd taken my anxiety meds (the maximum dosage) right before he'd called, and they had mercifully dulled my senses. Despite our impending proximity, right after a whole week of emotional rawness, my heart maintained a steady rhythm.

I wasn't nervous, anxious, sad—anything. I was tired, the kind of tired that no amount of sleep can erase. When I got back, Grant was sitting on the edge of the guest bed, head in his hands. I leaned against the doorframe, silhouetted by the light spilling in from the hallway and cleared my throat. "Hey. Do you want to sleep … with me?"

He hesitated, glancing up at me. "Why?"

"I'm just tired of being sad," I replied. "Aren't you? It would be nice to pretend … just for one night."

The resulting silence was only moments long, but consuming.

"No pressure. I'm going to take a shower." I turned, leaving him and hating the small bubble of hope that staccatoed in my chest. What did I want to happen? Any comfort we found in each other would be temporary. I was struggling with the breakup, but that didn't change anything. It didn't make living with it any easier. Post-shower, I pulled on a big tee and fitted, black shorts as I heard the floor creak in the hall behind me.

I held my breath, waiting, hoping, until he slipped into bed beside me. Waves of relief flooded my body. It felt good to snuggle up beside him, my cheek pillowed by his chest, his arm around my shoulders. It was a familiar position, magnified by the impending forever loss of it.

We were breaking every rule. I was self-sabotaging. I didn't care. All I wanted, after so many painful, sleepless nights, was to be held. To not be alone. To pretend. Since Grant had taken me up on it, I knew some part of him wanted that, too. We talked for hours, him mostly, me battling a drowsy, anxiety-medicated haze. I listened to his heartbeat—willing myself to cement the sound in my memory. The peace I found there, right there, was something I never wanted to forget.

Curled up in the dark, it was easy to forget how someone had hurt you. It was easy to slip back into the warmth and comfort of fitting together. It was easy to push off worry about how tomorrow might feel because, right then, this felt achingly good. As we attempted sleep, the air felt charged with our shared pain and unasked questions.

My meds had done a beautiful job of numbing anything I might feel, but I surprised myself when I asked him, "Is it okay if I kiss you?"

Grant was silent for a beat. "Why?"

Why indeed. It was hard to articulate between my drowsiness and the confusion of emotion rattling around inside my ribs. "To see if I still want to."

He mulled that over, both of us on our sides, facing each other, inches apart. "I only want you to kiss me if it means something."

I exhaled. "That's fair, but this changes nothing. I'm surprised I'm even asking, honestly." I paused. "It's more like … in the spirit of exploration." If I weren't so tired, I might have recognized the inherent flirtiness of this comment. But right then, I was worn out, tired of fighting for "what's best."

He inched closer, a familiar weight hovering above me as his opposite hand found my hair, fingers sinking into my curls. "I can get behind exploration."

Our kisses were slow at first, truly exploratory. I felt a little burst of shock that I was open to this at all. My heart felt like a shredded, gasping thing. I didn't care if this wound was lethal. Right then, I was desperate for even a band-aid—no matter how fleeting the relief would be. I could process this without strings attached. We were both consenting adults, right?

I'd forgotten how good the stubble of his beard felt against my skin. His kisses took a different energy. He felt hungrier now. I melted into him, my mouth soft, inviting, sighing as more of his weight pressed upon me. I felt the hardness of him against my thigh. This was the most doped up and frantic I'd ever felt. I reached for him, pulling him more on top of me.

"I am rock hard right now," he said, panting.

"I want to have sex with you," I replied breathlessly. We kissed again, a crush of a kiss that was eager and hungry as we started to paw at our own clothes. "But we both want this right now, right? We're both saying yes? This isn't something you'll use against me later?"

He stilled. "The fact that you're saying that means I really messed this up."

I didn't care about his emotional revelations. I was *aching* for him. I wanted him *now*. There was such eagerness to us both, a realization that we'd been given this "last chance" neither of us thought we'd have.

"Yes," he said at last, "I want to have sex with you, too."

I tore my shirt off. Our mouths tangled in fevered kisses. I paused to look up at him. My fingers clutched his shoulders, dragging down his back as he thrusted. *Here*, right here, I used to say I love you. Here, our joining used to mean something more.

Here, in this moment, I knew everything had changed.

I didn't regret it the next morning. There had been something soothing in his presence and exciting in the passion. I had felt comfortable, powerful, and … empty. So glaringly empty. I had taken the maximum dosage of my anxiety medication before this experiment, enough to totally knock me out. That could explain the numbness. There was a bottomless void inside of me in a place that had once been swollen with love.

It wasn't that the sex was bad. It wasn't. It had been energetic, frantic, forceful—like we could outpace our pain. Being held, being kissed, making love with someone still connected to me had felt like resurfacing in water when you're desperate for air. The crush of oxygen hitting empty lungs? Exquisite. But afterwards? In the dark, when we'd once again settled and curled up together? I felt empty. Sad. I could remember how much those moments had meant to me. Now we were extending a long goodbye. Our inevitable parting loomed large on our horizon.

I woke up early, left him sleeping, and sat drowsily on my couch with a cup of tea for an hour or two before he woke up and joined me. He sat beside me, hip to hip, an expression of physical closeness he'd always been a little hesitant about—but that he knew was my love language.

"Can we try something?" he asked.

I nodded, and he laid down on the couch beside me, resting his head in my lap. He asked if I could run my fingers through his hair, which I did, with a persistent clatter of panic that I tried to chase away. Empty. All of this felt ... rehearsed. Too late. I wanted to drown it all out. "Do you want to pretend, just for today," I asked softly, "that the breakup never happened?"

He looked up at me. "Yes, I'd like that very much."

IT WAS PALM SUNDAY. I asked him to come to church with me. We sat hip to hip again, my arm looped through his elbow. I made crosses out of the palms for us both like my dad used to do for me when I was a kid. We went to the movies after to see the new *Ghostbusters*. We snuggled for the whole thing.

It was mid-afternoon when we got back to my house. He gathered his things to go. It had been a lovely day, tinged with warmth and softness. It crawled to a close as he lingered in my kitchen, heading for the door. I'd allowed myself to freefall into the pretend of the breakup never happening. In those final moments, it all came slamming back. Grant paused, setting down his suitcase, when Digory came up to him for pets. Neither of us acknowledged it, my eyes remaining glued to the black-and-white tile floor, as Digory circled in delight before him.

I'd spent the last year documenting my firsts, but this, most assuredly, was a last.

The bitterness of that realization was inescapable, drenching every second of this goodbye. Even if we were friends after this, even if it was all right in the end, once he walked out that door, it would never be like this again. You don't always know when something is your last time, but I recognized it now. This was an ending.

My throat tightened, eyes watering, as he straightened. I pulled him into a tight goodbye hug, pressing my nose, one more time, into his neck. I still fit.

"Thanks for being there, when I called," he said.

"Of course," I choked out. I didn't add "always." Because it wasn't true, not anymore. I was drowning.

"I'll talk to you soon?" he asked.

I nodded, and then he was gone.

Grief swallowed me whole. I cried, hard, for hours. It felt like two halves of me shredding into unsalvageable pieces all over again. Knowing this breakup had been necessary didn't make it any less painful. I had shrunk myself to fit within the confines of our relationship and, even knowing I was making my world small, I still fought tooth and nail for it anyway. Then there was this soft, bruised part of me. The part that had relished his company, the comfort of his arms, the hunger in his kisses.

I'd wished that the love between us, fragile as it was, had been enough, but it wasn't.

I sent him a mushy text later, the kind that said I had no regrets, that I treasured our time together, that he still meant so much to me. He deflected, replying with a humorous response—something non-committal and witty. It felt like being doused with a bucket of cold water. *Of course* he wouldn't respond with mushy emotions.

At the end, he was willing to try again, to make it work. But it didn't change that we *didn't* work. It didn't change that we weren't right for each other. It didn't change that I wanted to live a bigger life than he'd wanted. It didn't change that I had begged, pleaded, to be loved, but just too early. He'd decided to love me too late.

Life returned to a crawl of unending agony, a monotony of minutes, hours, days. I regretted little in my life, but opening myself up to feeling love to have nothingness as a reward? There was nothing I regretted more.

Chapter 28

RELEARNING LIFE ALONE

The only way out from an emotional maelstrom is to go through it, to feel it, to let the emotions wash over you, and to learn how to put them behind you. Repeat that process as many times as needed through every low moment, every triggering memory, every deluge of despair.

That felt like shitty advice when simply existing in my body felt like an agony. I broke down one day because nowhere I slept was soft enough. My couch was too firm, the floor too hard, my bed too abrasive, the guest bed too unfamiliar. I cried over being exhausted and feeling like there was no respite, nowhere to go, no place where I would feel safe, happy, or loved again.

The Allora I was in 2022, who'd been thrilled with her life, travelled the world, found the courage to face her fears, and try dating one more time seemed grotesquely far away. This new Allora cried herself to sleep every night. Her grief rotted her insides. The pretense of saying "everything was fine" on TikTok eventually caught up with me. I couldn't stand even the most well-meaning questions asking when Grant and I would get married, how happy I looked, how sweet he was. I decided it was time to "go public" with the breakup, which resulted in another nasty fight a week later.

"I'm not going to drag you," I told Grant in a heated phone call. "But it feels like living a lie. I cannot live that way."

"There's no coming back if you do this," he told me. "The breakup is for real. There's no getting back together. It's our business. The world doesn't need to know it."

Both sentiments gave me pause. Of course, the breakup was *real*. It had been real from the moment I'd suggested it weeks ago. Did the world need to know every detail of my personal life? No. But I'd built my platform being as authentic and transparent as I could. Lying about it now, pretending everything was fine, rankled. I refused to do it any longer. In the end, he understood why I decided to put it all out in the open, but not before another fight. He intentionally said something hurtful to get under my skin—a familiar, angry pattern that had helped end our relationship in the first place.

This time, he accused me of using him by sleeping with him— the thing I'd sworn he'd better not use against me. We'd both been there, we'd both consented, and I did *not* deserve this guilt trip. I never did. No matter how many times he promised me he changed, how many times he promised this would never happen again, I still found myself here.

He apologized as soon as I pointed it out. He was sorry; he was always so sorry. It would be different this time. It wouldn't happen again. I suggested that we needed real time to heal, a proper no contact period. Hurt people, *hurt* people. We could meet up once a month to check in on each other. It felt more bearable, even after all the hurt, knowing we'd see each other again eventually. It felt hopeful, like maybe the pain wouldn't always run so deep.

In the weeks that followed, the things I missed the most lacked permanence: my chin tucked into his neck, inhaling the crisp scent of his aftershave, how he'd hold me when I cried, how he always tried to make me laugh when I was at my lowest. All I wanted was for him to show up at my door. I'd catch myself looking out the window for him as if he'd come striding up the front steps and right back into my arms. We'd hug. He'd hold me.

The weight of loneliness can be crushing, especially when you'd had a taste of something different after a lifetime without it. I *loved* being loved and being *in* love. I hated whatever this was now. I'd get these glimmers sometimes, moments when I was doing something and realized it was something we used to do together. I hated everything about this process of unmaking all that we had been to each other, drifting back to our corners of the world, our lives disconnecting as if they had never merged.

I wanted to let it all go—I needed to. The longing for him didn't mend what had gotten us to this point: the eroded trust, the parting of ways. It couldn't bring back the version of me who had entrusted him with my heart.

Our first post-breakup meeting took place on a sunny, Sunday afternoon in May. We met up in his hometown and took a walk along one of the canals. It had been good to see him, but my hands tremored from the moment we'd reunited. He made small talk—asking me about my writing, my family, what movies I'd seen. How could we exist like this? With a cool wall of politeness, but not familiarity, between us?

I made careful not to touch him or walk too close. My thoughts were scattered, a chaotic bubble of hurt, hope, and need. *How could he have let this get so ugly? Once, I'd felt safe when he held me. Why did we have to go through this? Don't touch me. Kiss me. Don't forget what I meant to you. Don't talk to me ever again.*

Tears burned in my eyes. We stopped at a park bench, haloed in warm, spring sunshine.

"I'm still so angry with you," I admitted, feeling hallowed out all over again.

He sighed, glancing once at his hands. "Sometimes, I'm still so angry with you, too. It will pass."

I hugged him goodbye, in the end, marveling at how I still wanted to fit there. We promised we'd reconnect next month.

I cried the whole way home.

I STARTED READING every self-help book, dating guide, or late bloomer memoir I could get my hands on. I felt like I was missing some integral part of myself—something I'd lost over the course of the previous year.

Who was I now? Why had I tolerated not fitting for so long? What was I desperately seeking in companionship that I hadn't been able to find on my own?

I inhaled lessons about self-love I wish a younger me had known, but an older me could adapt to from Devrie Donalson's *You're Going to Die Alone*.

I explored how trauma shapes us, changes us, but that we are responsible for our resulting actions from Zachary Levi's *Radical Love*.

I sought understanding of my anxious attachment pattern and how to become more secure in it—and myself—in *Attached* by Amir Levine and Rachel Heller.

I looked for new ways to rediscover happiness in my life with Stephanie Harrison's *New Happy*.

I learned how to set non-negotiables and how to look for them in a potential partner in Lily Womble's *Thank You, More Please*.

I learned about healthy communication skills, at any stage of dating or a relationship, with Therapy Jeff's *Big Dating Energy*.

I studied strategies for strengthening my own emotional and mental well-being, while also sifting "men from the boys" in my future quest to find a life partner in Chantal Heide's *No More Assholes*.

I learned how to protect my peace as a single person and live boldly *now* in Shani Silver's *A Single Revolution*.

I explored other late bloomer experiences in Treva Brandon Scharf's *Done Being Single* and Rebel Wilson's *Rebel Rising*.

I went to therapy, drowned myself in writing this book, surrounded myself with the company of family and friends. I cried my eyes out on the phone to anyone who would listen, picked up old hobbies, visited new parks and restaurants, tried new trails with Digory, visited my parents multiple times by the beach in sunny Delaware. All of it was in pursuit of rebuilding this new Allora—a version of myself who knew what it was to have been loved and to have lost it. I was figuring out what she needed and who she was after experiencing the sharpest heartbreak of her life, brick by emotional brick.

WE MET up a second time in June, this time at a bookstore café I'd never been to—Grant's suggestion. It was a short, one-hour meetup, in which I managed to keep the small talk going and focused solely on him. I didn't make it through that meeting without crying again, which I'm not sure he understood.

When we said goodbye, I didn't hug him.

"YOU SEEM LIKE YOU AGAIN," my bestie, Shay, told me over dinner one night in her home. "It's good to see you like that."

One night, fresh from the breakup, I'd told my out-of-state bestie, Erika, that I'd been listening to Louis Armstrong's "Smile" on repeat. Without warning, Erika had called Shay, who showed up at my door less than an hour later to check up on me. I was stunned by their concern. Shay was the one who scraped me off the floor as I tremored and sobbed in her arms during the big fight in November—my breaking point.

I'd been vocal about my mental health with both of my friends as the months progressed, but I hadn't realized how worried they'd been about me until that mayday visit. I'd honestly always considered "Smile" to be such a hopeful song, with its assurances of better days ahead. "I'm depressed," I snapped at Shay. "Not suicidal."

I knew, deep down, that they were looking out for me. I appreciated how much they both cared. To hear Shay tell me, in late summer, that I seemed me again felt like a full circle moment.

I was having more "good" days. Someone told me to keep a calendar marking my good days in green and the bad days in red. "So you can look back and literally see when the good days outnumber the bad." I took them up on it. Within a few months post-breakup, I'd had plenty of good days, so long as I did nothing that reminded me of Grant.

During my mid-year reviews at work, my boss told me, "You

seem the happiest this year, personally and professionally, that I've seen you in a while. Your work has been exceptional."

This struck me as ironic because there had been days that I'd spent my lunch breaks curled up in a ball on my couch, sobbing my guts out, only to dust myself off and give the performance of a lifetime when I signed back in for a meeting.

Everywhere I turned, there seemed to be more signs, slowly but surely, that I was finding my way back to me. A little by brute force, a little by letting myself feel all the feelings and cry them out, a little by surrounding myself with love, a little by seeking to understand and better myself.

I was finding my way back to happy.

I hadn't realized, until then, that I'd gotten so lost.

THERE WAS a gradual shift in how Grant and I treated each other post-breakup. I still felt angry and hurt. Had he been a terrible person? Absolutely not. But I'd gone into our relationship with no walls and my heart laid bare. And, ever so slowly, trust eroded. Walls went up. Although there had been many attempts to course correct, we always seemed to fight about the same things over and over.

What started as an amicable breakup soured as time went on.

Why are you even sad? he texted me at one point. *You're the one who broke up with me.*

Yes, I had. I'd broken up with trusting him, loving him, building dreams for our future together. I'd broken up with a life I'd known wasn't enough for the hope of having a different one, with someone else who fit me better, in an unknown future. My continued distance and sadness frustrated him. He wanted his sunshiney best friend back.

I was frustrated that he expected me to be over the most profound heartbreak I'd ever experienced, one that was layered with losing my sense of self, living alone, and struggling with my mental health for the first time. He expected us to jump straight into friendship, but I didn't know how to be friends without loving him.

Where did that leave us?

. . .

THE LAST TIME we spoke was to plan our monthly meetup—a conversation that went south fast, escalating to another bitter fight. At the heart of it, he was angry that I was no longer as kind, that I took too long to answer his messages, that he hadn't realized friendship and kindness from me were conditional.

I didn't realize until then that friendship with anyone could be conditional, but it was. My kindness, warmth, and affection were not infinite resources. They'd burnt out in fighting and failing to be loved the way I needed. I wanted to be friends with someone I trusted and who trusted me. In the end, that was the problem. There was no longer trust between us, and I didn't know how there ever could be again. I hoped there would be, but it was still too soon, the pain too fresh.

We traded volleys of sharply worded texts, mine curt and to the point, his bruised and aimed to hurt. He decided that I must be going insane and a was danger to myself. He threatened to call my parents.

I laughed. *Be my guest.*

I tried to call, and call again, in complete disbelief that this could be so ugly. Surely, if we could talk, we could work this out. He refused to answer my calls. He told me to leave him alone. He threatened to sue me.

I couldn't believe, after everything we'd been through, that it could be ending like this. I called Erika, sobbing. I didn't want to block him; I lacked the nerve. I knew it would hurt him. I didn't want to hurt him. But the words coming out of him were getting uglier with each successive text.

"You need to protect yourself now," she said. "He threatened to sue you. Hurt or not, nothing either of you say can help each other right now."

All my months of healing evaporated in an instant. I cried myself to sleep for the first time in months. This was his pattern, using barbed words to elicit a reaction. I recognized, early on, that this was unhealthy. It was a pattern he'd repeatedly promised to break. But there we were, five months after our breakup, repeating the same story.

I saw *Deadpool & Wolverine* after with my brother the next day. When we emerged from the theater, I found worried voicemails from my mom, saying Grant had called her saying that I was being "uncharacteristically mean" and that he was worried about me. I was livid. This was a gross overstep, a huge breach not just of trust, but of respect. Did he really think he could change the narrative of our relationship and breakup to *my own parents*?

I called my mom, recapping our recent fight, telling her about his threats to sue.

"You see now," she said, "it's dangerous to keep in contact with him."

I agreed he overstepped, but *dangerous? My Gentleman Caller?* He was many things to me, but not that. Never that. He couldn't be. I asked my parents to let him know they'd spoken to me, so he'd stop reaching out. My father took it a step further. He called Grant and left a voicemail when he didn't answer. "We talked to Allora. Do not reach out to her again. If you feel the need to do so, you can contact me first."

I was both relieved and embarrassed that my parents had stepped in. I was a big girl; I should be able to handle my own drama. But here my dad was, swooping in to protect me. By dusk, my anger had fizzled, morphing into guilt. In the past, when we fought, he'd torpedo-text my phone with apologies. Maybe he'd panic when I didn't respond. Maybe he was worried. I unblocked him and sent him another text stating as much. I waited two days for a response.

He didn't respond.

I sent one final text:

I really held onto such hope the last few days that we would be able to mend things. Make peace. But hurt people hurt people. We have both been hurt. And we can't seem to stop hurting each other. I don't want our story to end this way. You are hung up on the fact that I used to be so sunshiney and kind, that I changed somehow. I'm not sure it occurred to you that sunshine and kindness are not an infinite supply. I wish it hadn't happened that way, but it did. And the hurt from what I wrote to you there still runs deep. I don't want to think of you poorly, but I also know I can't keep hoping for a happier ending for us. I don't trust you with my heart.

So you're right, we do need to say good bye. Maybe one day it will be different. Maybe one day we can be friends. I was never holding back rage during our meetups. I was holding back grief. I just wanted to sob every time I saw you. I wanted you to hold me. I wanted to kiss you. I wanted to never see you again. All of it was just this open wound of profound grief that I'd never experienced before. And I was angry because you just expected me to be okay. To just move on. But I have never loved anyone like I loved you. Even though I ended things between us, it doesn't mean I could move on so quickly. I shouldn't have gone to those meetups until that grief had passed, but hindsight right?

You made living here bearable in those first months. I will always think of how you made sure I was okay during our first kiss. How you'd look into my eyes when we made love and tell me that you loved me. How you'd hold me when I would shake. How you'd always try to make me smile, and so many beautiful firsts along the way. How you tried to be there for me during the darkest time of my life.

I don't want to think of the fights, the lack of trust, the pain. I want to always think of you as my Gentleman Caller. So that brings me to now. We need time for the hurt to pass. We pinky promised, right? That we'd never ghost each other if we broke up? That we'd peacefully go our separate ways? So this is goodbye. I can't change your mind if you want to think of me as an angry, crazy ex. As the villain in your story. But that's not how I'll think of you. I wish you every happiness this world has to offer. And I hope you also find the healing you deserve.

Goodbye, Gentleman Caller.

I found out later he texted my parents twice more in response instead of talking to me. He told them he thought the world of me and thanked them for being so welcoming. It didn't matter. It was the end of everything we'd been to each other.

I expected an emotional fallout all over again after that final showdown but, weirdly, it felt like a weight had been lifted. I hated the way we ended. It felt ugly. I tried to avoid this outcome, but I hadn't realized how having the pressure to get over my grief and be who *he* needed me to be was impacting me. I never stopped to ask, besides the breakup itself, what I needed for myself.

I'd told him, when we started dating, that the main way I showed love was through acts of service. I liked to take care of, in whatever way I could, the people I loved. I had worried that I'd lose myself in wanting to take care of him, silencing my own needs and desires as a necessary sacrifice to keep the peace. I had made myself smaller and smaller because relationships were about compromise, right? I hadn't realized how much I had been willing to give and how little I'd been willing to take in return. It scared me, a rude awakening that I'd allowed this ugliness, helped build it even, and it had taken every ounce of strength I had to walk away from it.

But now? I felt lighter than air. I couldn't change what past-Allora had done, hoped for, or allowed. But I could take what I had learned, grow, and evolve. I could learn to be stronger next time. I could learn not to lose *me* next time.

There was the certainty within me that there would be a next time. One day, I would try again. We all die alone, but I was determined not to live on my own. In the meantime, I had a lot of practice living life boldly, loudly, adventurously, on my own. I could do it again.

My life hadn't begun when I met Grant. It wasn't going to end now.

A MONTH after we last spoke, I knew it was time. I woke up one day, a few days before my 34th birthday, opened my phone, and began deleting all traces of him. Every photo. Every video. I kept a handful of printed pictures of us, hopeful that one day I could look back at them and remember better days.

I like to think I get closer to that version of myself all the time.

In the moment, it felt methodical. I drifted through each memory, relived it one more time, and let it go. I didn't cry. It felt like coming up for air, but my chest still felt tight. I wished for a hug, looking out the window for any sign of him walking up my driveway. Silly, right? To be completely ready to let someone go, while simultaneously mourning the loss of them in your life? Like I could strip away the memory of his skin against mine. The sharpness of every barbed word. The pain of losing my love for him.

I deleted it all, saving one voice memo he sent the day after we broke up for last:

I decided I wanted to do this before we officially parted ways. It was obviously a very tough day, and I spent a lot of time focusing on how hurtful it was for me. It hit me to realize that this is your first breakup ever, and you were very hurt; I could hear it in your voice. And it made me very sad, and I'm sorry that … that the conclusion that was reached was felt for the best. But I just want you to know that you're going to be okay.

Don't guilt yourself over this. You really helped me during one of the darkest times of my life. But thank you, for giving me a wonderful year, and so many wonderful moments. I don't regret them, and I want you to know that. And I want you to keep this in case, one day somehow, we just don't make it as friends. So you can have this, knowing you made a difference with somebody in their life. And I really mean that, Allora, I do. Okay, this is also probably the last one of these I'm going to send. Thank you. I loved all of it, and I love you for it. I really do. I will love you forever. Goodbye for now.

I KEPT GOING. There were plenty more "firsts" to be hand, but this was the last one I allowed myself to have with him: the first time truly letting him go.

Chapter 29

BEETLEJUICE, BEETLEJUICE

I'd see phantom memories of Grant from time to time, pacing beside my bed before we went to sleep or the feel of him pressed against me. For months, I'd reach over and touch the pillow he used, a leftover muscle memory. There had always been a flicker of awe every time my fingers would brush his shoulder, amazed all over again that I loved someone enough to be sleeping beside me.

Returning to solitude was excruciating. My loneliness was more stark and vivid in understanding what I'd lost. Memories lost their vibrancy and emotional weight the more time slipped by. It amazed me, how the things that haunt you the most become echoes in your past. The pain of loss became blunted as days, weeks, and months went by. Everyday tears became occasional misty-eyed moments. New memories replaced the old at places we'd once frequented together.

I started reading fiction again. I'd fallen out of love with reading the previous year, and I wondered, when it came back in a tidal wave post-breakup, if that had been a warning sign from my subconscious. A hint, even then, that I knew this relationship wasn't right for me long before it ended.

Every book I finished felt like piecing together a little more of me: the Allora who had been strong and brave enough to try dating in the first place after carrying decades of false starts and fears that made every attempt harder and harder to even begin. I was remembering what made me, *me*. It was a certainty I'd lost. But I'd changed.

I wanted to remember laughing with him, the butterflies in my stomach as we danced through every "first," my excitement, cuddles on cold days. I wanted to bubble-wrap those memories, but every sharp word that passed between us made it harder and harder to do.

I was different now. I understood what love and heartbreak felt like. I knew I was capable of doing things I'd never dreamed of. I discovered that at my lowest points, I had people waiting to pick me up and help me find my way. I found my voice. I pushed through my fears. It made all my dreams larger, more daunting, and more real at the same time.

Who is *she*?

ALMOST SIX MONTHS to the date of our breakup, I went to see *Beetlejuice, Beetlejuice* in theaters on my own. Michael Keaton was one of Grant's favorite actors, and we'd gone to see *Beetlejuice the Musical* on one of our early dates. I'd been dreading the release date ever since we broke up. I knew that, no matter what, it would be a sharp reminder of something we would have done together, of the something between us that no longer existed. The release day came and, instead of asking anyone to go with me, I decided to go alone.

There wasn't anything premeditated in that decision. I didn't go to prove that I was over him. I just had a free Friday night and didn't want to bug anyone last minute to come.

Every seat was filled. When I got to mine with my little soda and popcorn, the movie began to play. I felt … nothing. No wistfulness or crush of sadness. No lamenting that I was here alone. I knew he would have enjoyed it. I imagined the conversation we would have had about it. I thought he'd love the Batman merch being sold alongside Beetlejuice merch at the concession stand. I wondered if he'd thrown away the Batman wallet I gifted him last year. All of those thoughts lacked the sharp edges of grief. I wasn't devastated, just … thoughtful. I enjoyed the movie, never once feeling lonely.

It was pouring rain by the time it ended, a true and proper deluge. I was soaked by the time I got to my car. I heard somewhere that you get just as wet (if not wetter) when you run through rain. It's one of those facts I have accepted as truth without ever bothering to verify. So, I kept walking, getting wetter and wetter, singing bits of "Day-O," thinking about going to the public market for peaches tomorrow, and maybe grabbing groceries on the way home. I was halfway to the car when I realized I hadn't thought about Grant for several minutes.

I didn't feel anything. Not pain, grief, or sadness just the absence of feeling. Yes, he probably loved this movie. I had, too. I liked the thought of that, us living our separate lives, seeing it separately, and still being happy. I wanted us both to be happy. Even if we never spoke again, the me from two months ago would have never believed it possible for me to see that movie alone without sobbing.

I enjoyed it. I was okay.

"Okay" is such a small word, a teeny, nothing sort of descriptor. There had been many moments in the past year that I'd thought I'd never be okay again. That I'd never be happy again. Never be me again. I could work with "okay." I could turn that into a baseline for facing my fears, trying something new, or—who knows—even falling in love again one day.

I was okay.

I'd *made* it.

For now, that was more than enough.

Chapter 30

SURVIVING A BROKEN HEART

Going through a breakup, first or otherwise, is no small thing. There is, likely, a part of you justified in thinking nothing might ever feel right again. Grief, after all, isn't linear; it comes in waves. You don't need to get over it, but you do need to get through it. You might emerge from the other side drenched, winded—but you're still alive and breathing. When you've never experienced love before, losing it once you've had it might feel like the ultimate worst-case scenario. It's not. Here are a few things that helped me, personally, find my way.

- **Let Yourself Cry.** Let all that grief wash right through you. Regardless of if you initiated the breakup or not, how long your connection lasted, or how meaningful it was to your ex. Your experience was meaningful, in some way, to you—otherwise you wouldn't be grieving the loss of it. Don't try to hold those emotions in. Feel them, and then let them go.

- **Keep a Calendar.** Mark your good days with a heart and your bad days with an "x." Over time, you'll start to see more good days from bad. It's a great visualization for your healing progress, even if it feels like nothing has changed.

- **Go No Contact for Three Months.** Amicable breakup or not, you need time to heal from the loss of this person and the future you might have envisioned with them. You don't need to say goodbye forever (unless you want to), but every time you see their name on your phone screen or hear their voice, you are reopening the wound. Give yourself the gift of not thinking about them or your connection to them. Let yourself heal. You can try to get in touch with them after a few months, if that's what you want, but don't try to cheat this system. It doesn't work.

- **Sever Your Emotional Connection.** Similar to #3, delete or hide any reminders of them. If you aren't ready to delete photos and videos, put them in a hidden album on your phone/device. If you aren't ready to throw away mementoes of them, put them in a box and pack them away. Again, you are letting those emotional wounds scab over. Maybe one day you can look at those pictures and mementos without them hurting you. Right now? Give yourself a break from the emotional gut punch you feel every time you see something that reminds you of them.

- **Break Up Your Routine.** Try new foods. Read new books. Watch new movies. Volunteer at a shelter. Retry an old hobby or start a new one. Rearrange your room or living space. Visit a park, a museum, a store or restaurant you've never been to before. My point? There is still so much life to explore, and you need distractions! Break up your everyday routine and shower yourself with the distraction of newness.

- **Make New Memories.** Have friends or family nearby? Now's the time to make plans to see them. Let yourself laugh, vent, cry, or just be with other people you love and who love you. If you can, don't wait for the weekends. Schedule things mid-week after work, on your lunch, or whenever you can squeeze in some social time.

- **Revisit Favorite Places.** Those places you used to visit with your ex? When you're ready, if you're so inclined, try visiting them again on your own or with a friend. Make a new, pleasant memory to replace the old. This way you have a positive experience to associate with a location that still might be a grief trigger.

- **Write a List.** Regardless of who initiated the breakup, it did happen. Write a list of all the ways you were not happy or compatible with this person. This list is just for you, so don't be afraid to be petty or to dig deep. This is a firm reminder to yourself, one that you can revisit as many times as you need to, as to why this didn't (and wouldn't) work out with this person.

- **Get Treats.** You are surviving this. You deserve treats. That thing you've been wanting for yourself? *Get it.* The dress that looked cute? A sweet from your favorite bakery? New merch from a favorite fandom? That book you've been dying to read? You deserve a happy boost. Get it! Spoil your dang fine self!

- **Get Back on the Horse.** You've heard that saying, right? Get back on a horse when you fall off, so you're not afraid to try again next time? This same concept applies. I don't mean that you need to rush into the dating scene or another relationship if you don't feel ready. But when you are feeling more yourself, try to think of dates as a fun opportunity to meet new people, conquer your own fears, and get better at dating. Take the pressure off yourself for trying to meet your soulmate. Try, instead, to go into a date (or two, etc.) with the sole purpose of having a good meal, maybe some decent conversation, but, mostly, to prove to your brain that you aren't too afraid to try again. Who knows? You might even have fun.

At the end of the day, we can do hard things. We can try to love again. There's no reason your story can't change. That's one of the best parts about life: sometimes it can surprise you in the best ways when you open yourself up to try.

Chapter 31

THE START OF SOMETHING NEW

It was late September, ten months since I'd mentally fallen apart, six months since the breakup, two months since I'd blocked Grant, and one day since I decided I wanted to try something new. I felt like me again, but I had this nagging feeling that I was right back to where I was a year and a half ago. I'd fought tooth and nail to get to the Allora I'd been before Grant, or—at least—to the Allora who'd been brimming with sunshine and confidence. That Allora had been brave enough to shed her secret, her shame, and to try dating again. Now that I was here, I found myself tempted to sink back into the comfort and familiarity of single life.

But there was this other part of me, a loud part, who'd allowed her dreams to grow and change with her. Although I knew I could live a great life on my own, I also knew that, now, I didn't want to. I had developed a taste for a life shared with someone I loved. I didn't want to be afraid to try again.

On September 21st, I downloaded two dating apps, Hinge and Bumble, and decided to give it my all for exactly 30 days. If nothing promising was happening at the end of it, I'd delete the apps and try again next year. My goal was to go on at least one date. This time around I hated Hinge (too pushy for upgrades) and loved

Bumble (with its encouragement to make the first move). It felt like a grand experiment and gave me the illusion of control. I wanted to feel like I could do impossible things—like dating again—while scared.

I wanted to quit after one week. Few conversations felt like they were panning out and fewer people matched my conversational energy. No one person seemed particularly appealing from the rest. I was, however, a sucker for a 30-day challenge, and I hated the thought of quitting before my goal date. I pressed on, fielding as many as ten conversations (of varying effort on the recipient's part) at a time.

By the end of week two, ten conversations became three that progressed past favorite colors, movies, food, etc. to personal histories, hopes, and dreams.

Not a single one of them had asked me out. I complained to my mother about it during my weekly "life update" call. "I'm having good conversations, but no one is making any moves."

My mom snorted. "Well, maybe it's time to call bullshit. If they don't ask you out, why don't you ask them? You are in control of your own life, Allora."

Speechless, I could not think of a single compelling reason to disagree. I texted all three that night explaining, *I have a personal rule of only chatting with someone on a dating app for a few weeks before asking to meet up with them. It's too hard to care about someone you don't know. So I'm asking, would you like to meet up? Or shall we say this was lovely and go our separate ways?*

I may have girlbossed a little too close to the sun with this one, because zero dates turned into three when all of them agreed. I found myself going on three first dates in the last week of my dating challenge. When I showed my sisters my "roster," they initially referred to them by their jobs. The first was a teacher, the second a physicist, and the last an electrician.

"The last one looks like a teddy bear," one sister told me.

"I bet he gives good hugs," said another.

"The Bear" became the top pick for his wild, shoulder-length hair, kind eyes, and love of the outdoors and homesteading.

It almost felt like a competition for who would win my hand. It made it fun. I liked bringing my friends and family along for the ride. Most were partnered themselves by now, and all were excited for my impending escapades. It made it feel more real, exciting, and less anxiety-inducing as each date approached. Being open with my family, surprisingly, made me feel normal and included in a way I'd never quite experienced before, even with Grant.

I met the teacher mid-week at a local brewery. We shared a love of history. Our conversation was stimulating. I wasn't physically attracted to him though. At the end of a few hours, I realized I wasn't having a bad time, but I wasn't particularly interested in getting to know him better. I felt relieved when I got home and received a text from him saying the same thing.

The physicist invited me to a Sunday afternoon date at a trendy café. We ordered tea and chatted for hours about our families, hobbies, and favorite books. At the end, he asked for my number. I gave it to him, but I also let him know I was still meeting other people. He had been the most emotionally vulnerable of the three, but, even though we were the same age, he seemed young. Feeling mostly ambivalent, I decided it wouldn't hurt to talk to him a little more, but I wasn't excited.

At this point, I had only limited experience for first dates, but I was looking for this unique kind of energy. It was hard to explain. I'd felt it on my first date with Grant. I'd been thrilled by the prospect of getting to know him better. My body came alive during that first date, releasing a flirty side of myself I hadn't known existed. Maybe that's what "sparks" are? I didn't know.

There was clear favoritism for the Bear as our first date approached. I thought he looked different—rugged—in a way that stood out on the dating apps. Although our conversations, thus far, had been pleasant, they'd also only been surface deep—nothing real or vulnerable. I couldn't figure him out yet. What I did know was that he was hard-working, forthright, upbeat, and he matched my conversational energy by asking and answering questions. He also ended every sentence with an exclamation point, which oddly made him seem like a permanently sunshiney person.

I wanted a bit of sunshine from someone else, and I was curious about what he'd be like in real life. He suggested we meet at a small café, but he had to reschedule when his car broke down just as I pulled into the café parking lot. I texted my parents to stand down. For safety's sake, I'd shared my location with them and asked if they could keep an eye out for me if I didn't text after a pre-established check in time.

Fabio is missing out, my dad texted back.

I'm gonna give him one more shot, I replied.

We picked a new night a few days later, after prolific apologies on his end and a suggestion for us to meet at a fancy Italian restaurant as an alternative. We met on October 21st on an unseasonably warm last day of my dating challenge. Temperatures soared to the high seventies, a rarity for upstate New York. Park Ave in Rochester was alive with activity and bustle for that surprise summer's day.

I wore a red, sleeveless sundress, with my hair styled big and curly. I parked farther down the street, walking up to the restaurant that looked packed, with tables and chairs spilling out onto the sidewalk for diners to enjoy dinner in the warmth and sunshine.

I spied him standing outside as I got closer, scanning the street for me, hands in his jean pockets, with thick, muscled arms, broad shoulders, and long, dark hair tied up in a manbun. I expected him to be kind, but I hadn't expected him to be so handsome. I raised my sunglasses for a better look. I knew from his profile that he had blue eyes, but I was unprepared for the brightness of them as he turned to look at me, silhouetted by a sunset glow. A smile creased his bearded face. He was a full head and shoulders taller than all the guests and waitstaff milling about.

I went in for a hug, like I had for my other dates, but this time, as he folded his arms around me—even briefly—I realized I wasn't nervous. I felt … *giddy.* I wasn't scared or intimidated, I was excited.

"They've got a table waiting for us," he said, gesturing with an open palm for me to lead the way. I stepped inside, following the hostess up a set of stairs to a small corner table by a window. I sashayed, my hips swaying side to side, as I crested those steps—aware of him behind me. Watching.

He ordered a whiskey. I ordered sangria. We skipped an appetizer, but had delicious meals (bison meatballs for me and steak for him). Conversation was lively and bubbly, bouncing between us. We dove into a whole range of topics, our dreams, hopes, pasts, families. He also owned a home but dreamt of owning land and homesteading—something that resonated with me after moving to the suburbs. He was chatty and friendly. He smiled easily and laughed often, loudly. His voice was deep, warm, jolly. I was excited to hear his answers and his questions. It was a Monday night, and I was sad when I realized the date was coming to an end.

I offered to split the bill, but he declined. "I asked you out so, really, I should cover this."

"Well *technically* I gave you an ultimatum and made you ask me out."

He smirked, sliding his card onto the bill. "I didn't see it like that. I was going to ask you out anyway."

My cheeks flushed.

He walked me to my car even though we'd parked on opposite ends of the street. The sun had set, but Park Ave was partially illuminated with a hazy, orange afterglow. The sky was a bruised sort of pink.

We stopped under a streetlight beside my car. He rocked back on his heels, took his hair down, tucked it behind his ears. I wondered, as butterflies fluttered behind my ribs, if he was nervous, too. I realized that I didn't know what should happen next. A wild part of me had truly enjoyed that date. I wanted to go on another with him. More startlingly, I wanted him to kiss me.

I began to babble. "Listen, I had a really lovely time tonight. I'd like to see you again. I'll send you my number. I'm deleting Bumble at midnight so, you know, send me a text if you ever want to talk to me again. But I don't want to put you on the spot." It all came out in a jumble. I hadn't paused long enough for him to even respond.

He shook his head. "You're not putting me on the spot. I'd like to do this again, soon. I'll text you."

It didn't matter how warm outside it was, I felt cold after he let me go from another hug, like my skin missed his touch and how he folded his body around mine. My head was filled with a single, clear thought: *FUCK. YES.*

I watched him walk back down the street. I waved. He waved back before disappearing around a corner. There was an almost painful burst of hope swelling within me as I realized this was someone I wanted more of. I was fascinated by that feeling. Even if he never spoke to me again, I was thrilled that I could feel *any* of this again. I hadn't let fear overwhelm me. I'd tried again. That version of myself I'd been chasing? She was back. Even if this went nowhere, I felt like I was leaking pure energy and light. I felt like *me*.

I sent him one last message before bed, as promised.

Hope you made it home safe and sound. I seriously did have a lovely time tonight. Thank you for dinner. Here's my number, and I'd love to see you again soon. Like I said, I'm all done with these forsaken apps for this year. So if you'd also like to meet up again, I hope I hear from you. Regardless, have a lovely night.

I sent it off, deleted Bumble, and fell into one of the deepest, most peaceful sleeps I'd had in months. It didn't matter if he never texted me back. I'd be disappointed, but not crushed, because this wasn't about him. It was about me. I wasn't broken.

Who is she?

That high carried me well into the next day. I was mildly disappointed that the Bear hadn't texted me before bed, but who cared? It was out of my hands. If he wanted to, he would. I walked Digory, made breakfast, clocked into work at 8 a.m., and was surprised to see a text from an unknown number at 8:02 a.m. I froze, heart pounding, as I clicked the message open.

Good morning, Allora! I did make it home safe! I hope you did as well! Also, this is the Bear! I probably should have led with that!

You know the feeling you get when you start a really good book? You get a little glimpse of what's to come in the first few pages and something piques your interest. Something hooks you in, and lets you know this is about to be a great story. As I settled back into my chair, sitting cross-legged under a cozy blanket, it felt like that—like starting a brand-new story. This was only the beginning. I couldn't wait to see where this one led.

Epilogue

How Do You Not Become Jaded?

Writing this book, while grieving my first ever breakup, was insanity. Recounting first kisses, lost innocence, emotional highs and lows, recognizing that I was no longer in love with the first person I ever loved, all while mourning a relationship in real time was not the best idea I've ever had, but it was cathartic. When I shared my breakup thoughts online, I was unprepared for the outpouring of support and the number of people who asked if trying to be in a relationship, knowing how painful it can be now, was worth it.

It's hard not to look around at the sea of partnered people around you and wonder why you don't have this yet. *What am I doing wrong?* You might not be doing anything wrong. Dating is hard. What I had to learn was that no one was coming to save or find me. There was no knight on a white horse. The only person who could make any of my dreams come true was me, which also meant I was the only one who could keep trying. It sucks, but it doesn't mean you've failed.

Dating is wild. You're out there hoping to connect with someone, who's also looking for someone, and that your personalities mesh, your interests align, your life experience is complimented. There are literally so many ifs. When something didn't happen for me, I would internalize it, like, *I'm the problem. I'm not good enough.*

The moment I stopped looking at it as nobody wanting me, but instead that I have not yet found someone that I want, it started to ease that pain. It gave me hope. There's not a time limit on love. We **cannot** be late to our own lives, which means if we haven't found the right person yet, the opportunity doesn't expire until death.

YOU MIGHT BE READING this and thinking, despite my reassurances at the beginning, that this story did not have a happy ending. But here are a couple of things I want you to know:

- There is a pain inherent to any change in life. It's sort of the price of evolution. "Growing pains." If you are 100% content with your life right now, change nothing. But if you change nothing, nothing changes. *That is okay.* For years I built a life I loved as a single person. I thrived. As Shani Silver says, my life as a single person was not my "prologue." That's main character energy, babe! But there did come a point where I woke up and realized that the status quo was no longer enough. I wanted something different. Realizing that I wanted to change my life was terrifying. People are great at building comfort zones. But then you're faced with a choice: change nothing or find a scary adventure and be lured out of your hobbit hole. Either choice can be difficult, but you still have to make it.

- Going through a breakup leveled me in every possible way. I get why people want to run away or get bangs or rearrange their homes post-breakup. You are desperate to do anything to not feel the feelings you have. Worse, everything about your normal existence triggers you. But, even knowing that, it doesn't change how grateful I am for everything I did experience in my first year in love. That's another thing I learned with Grant: that it is okay to need and want something different. Being in a relationship made my dreams bigger, my hope more fervent. Even though it didn't work out, even though I had to fight for that future every step of the way, being in love made me want things I didn't know I was capable of wanting. I'll never regret that. I would rather try to love, then to not love (or be loved) at all.

- I understand the fear—especially for late bloomers—of having a chance at love, after waiting for it for so long, and then losing it. Know I have lived through your worst-case scenario. I am no one special, and I have survived it. It does get better. The sun does continue to shine. We can do hard things. We can make it through.

- It is a humbling experience to get exactly what you thought you wanted, only to realize it's not exactly what you *needed*. It's a hard thing to look at your life, at your choices, and recognize what is or is not serving you. It's even harder to take the risk to change it. I know now that we can do it. We can do hard things. We can do it scared.

In the end, I know this isn't the only adventure waiting for me. I know there will be storm clouds ahead, but I can weather them. I know rain can only last for so long. I know what it is to dream, to love, to grow, to survive, to evolve. I know what it is to find yourself when you thought you were lost. Call me cheesy, but I think that's the happiest ending of all (for now), until I'm ready to find love again.

I'll never stop rooting for us all to achieve what sets our souls on fire. I'm hopeful for the future. Are you?

Good lord, who is *she*?

Follow Allora Online

Sign up for Allora's Newsletter at:

https://alloradannon.com/newsletter

Join our late bloomer support group on Facebook:

http://bit.ly/3U7mgtk

Acknowledgments

I've dreamed of publishing a book since I was a little girl—feverishly writing *Lord of the Rings* fanfiction while hiding in trees because I thought my enthusiastic storytelling was illegal. Since then, publication has always felt like such a faraway dream, and writing these acknowledgements now feels wild. Thanks little me, you freaking nerd, for never giving up.

All that to say, I absolutely have to thank:

My parents, for supporting me and my creative passions every step of the way (even when they didn't necessarily love my execution of them).

My siblings, for continuing to be the most wonderful group of people on the planet. I've loved becoming grownup friends with you all as you (mostly) stop being so little and annoying. I've loved you all a LONG time, and I'm honored to be your big sister. You all helped make me who I am today.

My soulmates, Erika and Shay, for being perpetually in my corner, for being the best hype crew, and for picking me up every time I've fallen down. You are both a part of my family, forever a part of my story, and I love the ever living daylights out of you both. Words will never be enough.

Ellie, thank you for half-my-life of friendship, for helping me find my writerly voice, and continuously trying to smooth out the rough edges of my worst writing habits.

Erica, for every writing check-in, every brainstorm, and for cheering me on when I wanted to give up. This book exists, in part, because of you!

Maggie, for leading a writing experience that changed me

forever. I figured out what I needed to let go of, and I'll never forget your part in it.

My OG "five followers," for still watching the content I was sure no one was seeing. Ya'll are the real ones!

Every single incredible person who has followed my journey on TikTok. You literally helped me find my voice and change my life. You are forever a part of my story now.

All the generous souls who helped me outfit my ENTIRE kitchen when I moved into my first home. I think of you all every day. I kept every note you included with your gifts.

The late bloomer community that has blossomed (pun intended) on TikTok. You are helping heal so many hearts by just contributing your voices. I'm so happy we found each other.

Eliecia at Eliecia Young Photography for the most stunning author headshots and cover shots. You captured my vision for this book perfectly.

Adam, for being the most patient and innovative editor. Thank you for seeing something in my story and for polishing it up into a masterpiece (one pesky adverb deletion at a time).

The Carpe Vitam Press team for making this book a reality!

Last, but not least, the Bear, for fixing what you didn't break and showing me the joy, hope, and possibility that exist from loving you and being loved by you… but that's a story for another day.

About the Author

Allora Dannon received her MA in Creative Writing and has previously published short fiction in *The Summerset Review, Pennsylvania English*, and *The Sonder Review*. After her late bloomer confessions accidentally went viral on TikTok, she dedicated herself to ending late bloomer stigmas and normalizing beginning to date at any age. She is a proud nerd, dog lover, and fantasy fan who's lowkey obsessed with happy endings, adventures of any size, dragons, gardening, and Elvis. This is her first memoir.